No BURNING BUSHES

Kathy Marotta

CREATION HOUSE
A STRANG COMPANY

No Burning Bushes by Kathy Marotta
Published by Creation House
A Strang Company
600 Rinehart Road
Lake Mary, Florida 32746
www.strangbookgroup.com

Unless otherwise marked, all Scripture quotations are from the Holy Bible, New International Version of the Bible. Copyright © 1973, 1978, 1984, International Bible Society. Used by permission.

Scripture quotations marked NKJV are from the New King James Version of the Bible. Copyright © 1979, 1980, 1982 by Thomas Nelson, Inc., publishers. Used by permission.

Scripture quotations marked THE MESSAGE are from The Message: The Bible in Contemporary English, copyright © 1993, 1994, 1995, 1996, 2000, 2001, 2002. Used by permission of NavPress Publishing Group.

Scripture quotations marked NLT are from the Holy Bible, New Living Translation, copyright © 1996. Used by permission of Tyndale House Publishers, Inc., Wheaton, IL 60189. All rights reserved.

Scripture quotations marked CEV are from the Contemporary English Version, copyright © 1995 by the American Bible Society. Used by permission.

"The Starfish Story" originally appeared in Loren Eiseley's *The Unexpected Universe* (New York: Harcourt, Brace and World, 1969).

Design Director: Bill Johnson
Cover design by Justin Evans
Photographs by Kathy, Mike, and Zack Marotta

Copyright © 2010 by Kathy Marotta
All rights reserved

Library of Congress Control Number: 2010939118
International Standard Book Number: 978-1-61638-272-8

First Edition

10 11 12 13 14 — 9 8 7 6 5 4 3 2 1
Printed in the United States of America

This book is dedicated to

My husband, Mike, and son Zachary

With Love

CONTENTS

Summer/Fall

Fall/Winter

ACKNOWLEDGMENTS

THERE ARE SO many people to thank for this book coming to fruition. First and foremost, I would like to thank my God in heaven. I praise You for Your incredible faithfulness and Divine Providence. Never would I have believed, for more than half of my life, I would be sitting here today in incredible awe of what You could do with so little. I had nothing to give You but my love and my obedience. I listened and I waited and You were there. You have equipped me to fight the battles of spiritual warfare, which often seemed to sabotage my attempts to glorify You through the words I prayed You would give me in the pages of this book. You are an awesome God. Words are not sufficient. So, I count on You to know the meditations of my heart and how great my love is for You.

I also need to thank my greatest supporters, my husband, Mike, and my son, Zack, the loves of my life and the inspirations for many of my stories. I consider myself blessed to have such a rich family life, so full of love. You believe in me even when I don't. I appreciate your patience, your tolerance, and your unwavering optimism. To my friend, Diane, you are a jewel. You are the essence of grace and have a capacity for honesty and authenticity that is always refreshing. I have appreciated your positive feedback and edits. Thank you to Jeanne Potter, my sweet friend, who edited my first devotion for this book, and to Leland Holder, photographer extraordinaire, for sharing your craft with me. A big thank you to my dear friend, and spiritual mentor, Jean McGarrity, who suggested I write a book several years ago. You are my champion. I don't know what I would do without your complete support in all that I do. To Lex, my friend, mentor, wise counsel, and so much more. You led me to Christ and taught me how to think outside the box. It is through the lens you gave me that I am able to write at all. I am forever grateful for our special friendship. And, finally, to my pastor, Jeff Henderson, who unknowingly reignited the flame in me to resurrect a desire to pursue my forgotten dream of writing a book. It was after one of Jeff's sermons, when he shared with his usual complete humility and transparency that I realized my previous pursuits were less about God and more about things of this world. A silent retreat soon after set my feet back on a godly path and the first entry for *No Burning Bushes* was penned. Thank you, Jeff!

Many other friends have inspired and encouraged me, too many to name, although I will try to hit the highlights: Kelly, my sweet neighbor; Laura, another neighbor; my brother, Allan; my Bosnia Teams; as well as, our brothers and sisters in Christ at the Evangelical Church in Bosnia who inspired several of the devotions. Thank you to Marjorie, a surprise blessing from God in my life. You are my friend and my sister in Christ. Your love for the Lord and unrelenting pursuit of him has enriched my life in more ways than you will ever know. My past and present small groups and women's Bible Study group, you have all helped me to grow in my transparency with others and with God. In the day-to-day troubles of life, you have been there for me, walked me through scripture, and given godly counsel, turning me back to the only One who can restore wholeness. I am nothing without my community of believers, who not only believe in Him, but also believe in me in ways I do not deserve. Yet, out of your love for others, you stand as incredible witnesses to what it means to "Love your neighbor as yourself." You have inspired at least a few stories, and I thank you for your living testimony in the everyday ordinariness of life.

INTRODUCTION

A S A LATE-BLOOMING Christian, I was in my thirties before realizing I had a jaw-dropping, three-hanky testimony. I know it is by the grace of God that I am here today writing these words. But, at the same time, I had never tethered all the details of my life together tracing God's hand in the whole thing. Ultimately, during a testimony series in adult Sunday school class, I was approached and asked if I would share my story. I prayed about it and, over a period of a couple of months, began to put my life's journey to Christ on paper, up until the moment I was sure it was He who had carried me out of the darkness to utter transformation. When I finally shared my testimony to a crowd of about fifty people, I was taken aback at the range of emotion. It was a blessing for me to compile my story into something I could share, a greater blessing to share it, but the response was both a blessing and also unsettling. Each time I have shared my story since then, I have felt the same tension. The unrest comes from those who, afterwards, approach me and share feelings of unworthiness, feeling their story is less exciting. Somehow, because my walk with, and to Jesus took such tragic turns, while others grew up without as much drama, left my audience feeling as if they needed a pivotal moment, a "Burning Bush," so to speak, to know unequivocally when God rescued them or appeared to them in the midst of their day-to-day existence. This was disturbing to me. It made me sad. While there is nothing about the first thirty years of my life that I would change, not the tragedy or the repercussions, not the mistakes of others or my own, I most certainly would not wish my tragic walk to Jesus just for any reader to feel a richer sense of their relationship with Him. It is for this reason, I have written, *No Burning Bushes: Discovering God in the Ordinary.*

During a drive down Jacksonville Beach, in a convertible with the top down, with my husband and our close friends, the Schiponis, I was discussing faith with my friend, Chris. She and I were discussing the very existence of Jesus manifested in our lives, when I believe the first seed may have been planted. In her endearing way of thirsting for more, she cried out, "I want my Burning Bush!" And so it is: the battle cry of us all. As we wage our own wars through life, we want assurance that God is in it with us. That He is who He says He is, and He is there in the fight.

I don't believe we need a "Burning Bush" story to recognize this truth in our lives. In this weekly devotional, it is my hope to paint a word picture, using creation as my canvas to illustrate God's presence in our lives everywhere, everyday. I believe we miss those moments because of busyness, temptation, pride, brokenness, un-forgiveness, fear, worry, the Enemy, and many other obstacles we allow to get in the way of a daily walk with our Lord and Savior. To rewrite my story would be too easy, so I'm telling bits and pieces of it in a different way. My goal is to take my reader on a walk, a walk with Jesus. We are all ordinary people, missing ordinary opportunities to witness an extraor-dinary God who is pursuing us, desiring to be with us, teach us, and love us, each moment of each day. We don't need a *Burning Bush*. Won't you walk with me and *Discover God in the Ordinary*?

Earth's crammed with heaven
And every common bush afire with God:
But only he who sees, takes off his shoes,
The rest sit round it, and pluck blackberries.
                    —Elizabeth Barrett Browning, "Aurora Leigh"

Winter/Spring

As water reflects a face, so a man's heart reflects the man (Prov. 27:19).

REFLECTION

Living Purposefully

As water reflects a face, so a man's heart reflects the man.
—PROVERBS 27:19

A NEW YEAR. SUCH pressure we place on ourselves with all of the New Year's resolutions. Show of hands... How many "plan" to lose weight (go ahead, get those hands up there, no one can see you!)? I gave up on New Year's resolutions a long time ago. I prefer to look backward! I know, I know. Everything and everyone tells you, "The past is the past. Don't look back." But, to me, it is the only measure I have of, "How am I doing?" It is somewhat of a barometer. If I like what I see, I can continue in the same direction. If I do not, I need to make some changes.

I choose reflection over projection. As opposed to making a list of "gotta do's," I ask myself a lot of "did I do's?" "Did I love much?" "Did I pray continually?" "Did they know I was a Christian by my love?" "Did I carry another's burdens?" "Did I love my neighbor as myself?" "Did I not love so much with words or tongue, but with actions and in truth?" (See 1 John 3:18.) "Did I show compassion and forgiveness?" "Did I encourage and serve?" "Did I show fear or did I trust, believe, and have faith?" "Did I speak the truth in love?" "Did I seek wisdom?" "Did I listen?' and, most importantly, "Did I love the Lord, my God, with all my heart, and all my soul and all my mind?" (See Matthew 22:37.)

These are the tasks God has called us to do. All of a sudden, dropping a few pounds looks a little less daunting to me. Of course, we will never fulfill these scriptures perfectly, but it is the barometer to which we must strive to meet each day. That is plenty for me. And, I find each year, there is room for improvement.

Let's not get confused though. This is not a deeds-based faith. We are saved by grace. Striving to be better by reviewing my "Did I Do" list is because I desire to be a better Christian, just as losing weight is something I desire come swimsuit season. The difference is God wants me to be a better Christian too. He knows how fulfilling a life of service, gratitude, love, compassion, wisdom, patience, and freedom from fear will be. And, I long to become who He has designed me to be, out of sheer gratitude for the incredible sacrifice He made for me in Jesus. At the beginning of each year, in fact, every day of the year, I need to be able to gaze at my reflection, both literally and figuratively, and like what I see. What still needs pruning, I will lift up to the greatest Gardener. It is enough for me. It is enough for Him.

As I enter another year, I think about the day. "This is the day the Lord has made, let us rejoice and be glad in it" (Ps. 118:24). It could be my last. I will rejoice in it. I think about the year. It could be my last. I will rejoice in it. I stand beside a Koi pond taking stock of my year in reflection and notice my own in the water as a beautiful fish enters the frame. Do I recognize the face looking back at me? Does my reflection capture my heart for Jesus? "As water reflects a face, so a man's heart reflects the man." (Prov. 27:19).

Holy One, You have graciously given us another year, entrusting us with more time. More time to do Your will, to be used by You. Help us to choose wisely, love lavishly and be wonderful witnesses of Your grace and sovereignty. Groom us and mold us according to Your will. In Jesus' name we pray, amen.

Weekly Wisdom Walk

Do you make New Year's resolutions? If so, how successful are you at completing them by year's end? If you are like many who abandon resolutions before the groundhog sees his shadow, consider making a questionnaire for yourself. Sit alone with God and think about what He might ask you, if today was your last day, or this year your last? Sift through Scripture and find some verses that resonate with you, key verses to live by, which might be a reach or challenge for you. Perhaps they are relationship related or financial. The Lord only asks that you "act justly, and to love mercy and walk humbly with your God" (Mic. 6:8). Do so this week, and in your walks with Him, go deeper in your relationship, listen and seek His truths and will for your life. There are many scripture references in today's devotion. Search them and ponder them in your heart or find some of your own. Make His Word your daily bread and hide His Word in your heart. Let these become your New Year's resolutions. There are none more meaningful and life giving.

There should be no division in the body, but that its parts should have equal concern for each other (1 Cor. 12:25).

THE CHURCH

One Body

But God has combined the members of the body and has given greater
honor to the parts that lacked it, so that there should be no division in the
body, but that its parts should have equal concern for each other. If one part
suffers, every part suffers with it; if one part is honored, every part rejoices
with it. Now you are the body of Christ, and each one of you is a part of it.
—1 CORINTHIANS 12:24–27

HAVE YOU EVER struggled with your church? Not the building, but the
people?

Paul's letter to the Corinthians speaks clearly about who we are as
the "body" of Christ. With this metaphor, he describes the way we, the church,
all work together and cannot function separate and apart from each other, just
as an eye or an ear cannot operate apart from our head. With great eloquence
Paul unravels a metaphor a child could understand.

Over the years, I've heard sermons and lectures about the "one body and its
many members." I have listened to Bible scholars and Sunday school speakers
unpack the message of how we are each different, but yet one in Christ—a
message of unity and inclusiveness. Why then can we so often be divisive?

Like so many verses in God's Word, His love letter to his Bride, I believe
we have skimmed over some of it to get to the good parts. The passages that
we believe apply directly to us. Not fully understanding that it all applies to
us. Maybe we are the mouthpiece or some other "presentable part" in our
thinking. Leaders in our churches, we are overscheduled and overcommitted
at the expense of our own undoing, all for the sake of Christ? We are teachers,
administrators, missionaries, caregivers, the first to sign up, and the last to

leave. We understand, "if one part suffers, every part suffers with it," or at least we think we do. So, we are good and faithful stewards and sometimes, find ourselves embittered towards those who do less. We've missed the point.

In Paul's letter to the people of Corinth, an eclectic crowd to be sure, constantly fighting off the wages of sin, he also mentions the weaker, the less-presentable and less-honorable members of the church body—those parts of the body we are modest about. Those we cover. In a stroke of his quill, he draws his comparison to those in the church of whom he speaks—the poor with only meager tithes to bring, the despised, and the less prominent. Maybe in our churches today, it is also those with little to offer, the weak, the lost, the broken. These are precisely the ones whom Jesus sought out when He came. Perhaps they are not winning souls for Christ, but they are making the first step. They are coming to the foot of the cross, surrendering what they have, all they have, in obedience and utter surrender, while others go about their faithful service quietly wondering whether their tithe is getting too big and inwardly questioning when these "less-honorable" members are going to pull their weight in service or wondering why they struggle to practice Biblical teachings as "perfectly" as they. At no point do we realize that we, too, are the broken ones. We are the lost, the weak.

And, so the division begins. Honor has been lost. There will be no rejoicing. Like the wisps of cirrus clouds making a spectacle of themselves one evening, decorating the sky above with vivid colors, each one was different. As a peculiar tufted puzzle, it seemed to fit together in perfect unity, yet there was a margin of space between them. Each one had a gift all its own, different and unique. Some were large and prominent, some small and meager—each befitting their place, leaders and followers, from boisterous crimson to melancholy blues. Incredible to watch as they moved together with shafts of light, passing through them against a setting sun. But, the light quickly faded, and the clouds began to separate. The vibrancy disappeared, replaced by grey. Each tufted gift faded, floated away. Some completely disappeared, dissolved, absorbed by dark night sky. And so it can be with us, if we do not keep our hearts, minds and thoughts set on the whole truth of God's Word. We are the church, the body of Christ. One body, made up of many members—those who do outwardly and those who do inwardly. Those who give a lot and those who give all they can. The privileged and the poor and everyone in between.

Honor each other. Honor the whole and you will honor God.

Heavenly Father, You are an incredibly faithful and patient God. Help us to model this character with others. Teach us Your ways.

Pour out Your truth to us through scripture, Your truth, not ours as we see it, read it or hear it from others. Let Your words be the ones we obey. Instill in us a thirst to know what it means to be a follower of Your son Jesus Christ. Give us the humility and the modesty to know Him and be known by Him in new and powerful ways. Teach us to be gracious, Lord, with others, not just when it is easy, but when it is difficult, especially then. Help us to be the church you intended us to be. In Jesus' precious and Holy name, amen.

WEEKLY WISDOM WALK

Spend some time this week in the Word. Read 1 Corinthians 12:12–21 "One Body, Many Parts." Continue searching for references to the Church as a body of believers. Take notes. Ask yourself some critical questions about your own church experience. Bring those questions to God in prayer this week. Journal anything that comes from your time in reading, reflection, and prayer.

For what is seen is temporary, but what is unseen is eternal (2 Cor. 4:18).

TREE HUGGER

Community

Therefore we do not lose heart. Though outwardly we are wasting away,
yet inwardly we are being renewed day by day. For our light and momen-
tary troubles are achieving for us an eternal glory that far outweighs
them all. So we fix our eyes not on what is seen, but on what is unseen.
For what is seen is temporary, but what is unseen is eternal.
—2 CORINTHIANS 4:16–18

M Y HUSBAND, MIKE, is a card-carrying tree hugger. We affectionately
referred to him as our "tree hugger" long before he actually found
a window sticker, which now adorns his car, stating as much! I
believe he loves trees most in the winter. Many people probably think of winter
as the gloomiest time of year, when everything is dormant and dead, but not
my husband. Without the canopy of foliage to hide the beauty of the gnarled
branches lying beneath, he is able to really appreciate the magnificence of every
tree, from the "Charlie Brown" trees to the grand majestic trees hundreds of
years old. The more character, the better. It gives him great joy, and while we
tease him relentlessly about this, I have to admit, he has slowly passed on his
love of God's creation to my son and me.

I am not a tree hugger yet, nor am I a gardener; however, I am told winter
is of critical importance to the growing season. Roots dive deeper into the soil,
while sap delves deeper into the soul of a tree, preparing it for another cycle
of growth. What we see on the surface is not the whole story. Somehow, my
husband instinctively has an understanding about the soul of a tree, which I
simply do not. But, it occurred to me, there is an important metaphor about life
here, relevant to even the casual observer like myself.

Each of us have our own seasons of life, some are even cyclical. Books have been written about the January blues. In fact, I think I might have experienced them myself one year. After a season of going through the motions of life at a rapid pace, falling behind in my spiritual disciplines, beginning to internalize a lot of struggles, and trying to handle things under my own strength instead of by God's grace and power, I soon found myself wrestling with darkness—in the gloominess of winter. For a brief period, I lost sight of the tremendous light emanating, not only in winter but also from inside of me. God will "bring to light what is hidden in darkness," (1 Cor. 4:5) so it is for this revelation that I prayed. I also prayed for the authenticity and humility to share it amidst a community of believers and bring these struggles that were crippling me before my Lord and Savior.

In just two days, my prayers were answered. Like the community of faithful believers in the Gospel of Mark, it was as if my Christian friends took my mat and lowered me, in my paralytic state, through the roof of Capernaum and lay me before Jesus. Without a second thought about the earth, thatch, and tile in His hair, Jesus forgave me of the sin of separation from Him—of trying to handle things under my own power. Then, he healed me of my affliction, so I could "walk" again, *with* Him. The entire experience was a blessing to me. On the surface, what first looked like gloom became a deep introspective prayer. Quickly, the prayer led to the brokenness I needed to experience the authenticity, which resulted in a tremendous experience of Christian community. All of this led me to move deeper into my relationship with the Lord and to, once again, fully acknowledge what it truly means to know Him as "Savior."

For this season of life, I was like the tree. What was happening on the surface of winter was not the whole story. I think we must all experience these tiny *deaths to self* in order to fully experience God's grace and be transformed, readied for the wonders to come. I am forever grateful to my mat bearers who placed me at Jesus' feet. What an extraordinary act of faith! I am also incredibly inspired by my husband, who is always an amazing example to me of how Paul instructed the Corinthians to *"fix our eyes not on what is seen, but on what is unseen. For what is seen is temporary, but what is unseen is eternal"*

> *Lord, help me to keep my eyes fixed on you always. And, when I stray, when I am tempted to take control by what I see, remind me of what is unseen. Remind me of the tree and of you, Lord. Let this be a metaphor for me to want to go deeper into relationship with you during times of struggle, knowing it is where I will find the nourishment and deep roots I need. In Jesus' precious and holy name, amen*

Weekly Wisdom Walk

Are there areas in your life where you are relying on your own strength instead of God's power? Jesus said, "For my yoke is easy and my burden is light" (Matt. 11:30). Is this true for you? If not, ask the Lord to reveal that, which needs to be surrendered to Him. As a reminder, continue to do this each time you see a magnificent tree this week!

May the God who gives endurance and encouragement give you a spirit of unity (Rom. 15:5).

TEAM SPIRIT

Unity

May the God who gives endurance and encouragement give you a spirit of unity among yourselves as you follow Christ Jesus, so that with one heart and mouth you may glorify the God and Father of our Lord Jesus Christ.
—ROMANS 15:5–6

HAVE YOU EVER been part of a team? Maybe you were asked to join a church committee or perhaps you are a teacher, a member of the faculty. Athletes aren't the only ones called to experience the team dynamic. The corporate arena is inundated with opportunities to work in unison with others who have different skill sets to work toward a common goal. This is the intriguing part to me, the differences. One might hope that those joined together to form a unit pursuing a common goal might share similarities, creating cohesiveness from the start. Yet, it has been my experience this is seldom the case.

Think of it, a football team would hardly be effective with eleven running backs, not one good wide receiver or quarterback among them. The same principle holds true for a choir or band, teachers, or corporate teams. We need the visionaries and the dreamers, the pragmatists and the realists, the listeners and the mouthpieces, the leaders and the followers; they all play a part. Separately, there may be discord in their setting, but brought together, particularly when there is a realization of the gifts they bring, harmony can evolve.

The keys to experiencing this unity and balance, is in knowing what you bring, knowing what you offer, and knowing what you do not. Recognize your gifts as well as the gifts of others, where yours end and theirs begin. Most of all, we must recognize all gifts are God given and to be used to glorify Him. When we serve God as a team, in this sense, we are acting as the church in the world, one body many members, each reliant on the other.

As my family and I were driving through the country, we came across a picturesque site. It was a rusty old shed, doubtfully used for anything anymore, barely standing next to the gnarliest, yet distinguished old tree, not a leaf upon it. Covering the ground was the intimation that spring would soon arrive in a widespread patch of daffodils, their brilliant yellows spectacular against a backdrop of winter grays and rusted metal. Deep in the meadow, these elements fixed themselves, intertwining each other with a sense of belonging. Apart from one another, there was no story to tell, but together in harmonious splendor, they were a team, not detracting from the next, but adding to it.

The effervescent yellow blossoms were so positive and upbeat, with nary a clue how short lived her contribution would be to the team, a jolt of color to get things started. The old shed, once good for nothing, now a support for the vines, which would cross through him, remnants of which still dangled beneath the roof. He was a battered and rusty spectacle, but his incredible support of the vines to come were only secondary to the crotchety wisdom of the tree, hundreds of years old, now leaning her heaviest branches on his rooftop, propping up the old girl. The soon-to-come spring leaves would render her heavy, calling many tiny creatures and birds to nest in her comfortable branches. They always make her feel useful and needed, despite her being well on in years. She is so grateful for her team. Are you? "May the God who gives endurance and encouragement give you a spirit of unity among yourselves as you follow Christ Jesus, so that with one heart and mouth you may glorify the God and Father of our Lord Jesus Christ" (Romans 15:5–6).

Gracious Creator God, You are Sovereign over all. How incredibly You have made each and every one of us. Help us to recognize the gifts You have given us and to realize they are God given, entrusted to be used for Your glory. Teach us to see these gifts in others and to acknowledge them, particularly when asked to serve on a team. Let us always appreciate the differences of others and celebrate them. Give all of us the ability to live harmoniously with each other and impart Your strength, encouragement, endurance and willingness to do so. In Jesus' precious name, amen

Weekly Wisdom Walk

Read Romans 14:1–15:13 "The Weak and The Strong." Give yourself a spiritual "check up" this week. How are you doing in relation to all Paul has to say about how we should act and accept our brothers and sisters? Think of the groups and teams you participate in or on. Is the group thriving? Why or why not? Are there any principles from the reading, which you can apply to your experience? Pray about what you have read and ask God to reveal any truths that might improve your walk with Him. Have a great week!

The Lord does not look at the things man looks at. Man looks at the outward appearance, but the Lord looks at the heart (1 Sam. 16:7).

Week 5

PICTURE PERSPECTIVE

Worldliness

The Lord does not look at the things man looks at. Man looks
at the outward appearance, but the Lord looks at the heart.
—1 SAMUEL 16:7

IN 2008, I returned from a mission trip to Bosnia, my first. Not just my first
trip to Bosnia or my first mission trip, it was both.

Fortunately for me, as these things tend to go, we went as a prayer team,
and we each had a role or roles to assume. Mine? I was in charge of the blog,
and I became the primary photographer. The former was a choice, the latter
became an instrument God used to teach me the lesson He taught Samuel. God
wastes nothing if He can use it for His glory and to edify His people!

Every day, we would go about our schedule and I would traipse a few paces
behind with my camera, trying to soak up every moment with these passionate,
resilient, and amazing people, all the while with my head on a swivel. I tried
to drink in the breathtaking vistas and absorb as much of the rich culture as
possible. Most captivating to me, though, was how this little partner church we
were visiting, was like an oasis in the desert of this joy and hope deprived, post-
war-torn country. All I could see was the juxtaposition of a church next to a
bombed-out home, or a flower bursting forth from rubble, a still-gutted factory
a block away from a brand new building, representing the rebirth of industry—
the duality, the contrast—it was everywhere. To my left, there were reminders
of war. To my right, I found expressions of a hope-filled future. Behind me,
hate; in front of me, love. Weeds... a perfect flower. At church, the only true
place where forgiveness had happened, smiling faces were found. Outside of
it—somber ones.

The images rushed through my mind day and night, and still do. Consequently, our blog was filled with these same images—the dark and the light. Unwittingly, it became a theme that undergirded my experience.

When we returned home, I suggested we all upload our photos to a website and combine our pictures to share with loved ones. It was then that I truly saw what the Lord wanted me to see.

There was another woman, Deb, on our mission trip. She has been going to Bosnia for years now and knows our friends there well. All of what I was experiencing was not unfamiliar to her. I knew she had different pictures than I had, because she tended to remember to have someone take the group photos. So, I was eager to see her uploaded album. Imagine my surprise to sit at my computer and watch her slide show. Not a single expression of war—not a blemish. Every shot captured the smiles and the hearts of the people and the joy of our experience there.

Before I had viewed the photos, I had asked my husband, "I wonder if you return to a place like Bosnia, do you ever stop seeing the bullet-clad school building?" In his infinite wisdom, he responded, "Yes, but I think that is a good thing. I think that's when you start really connecting and seeing the people." I loved that point of view. I pondered it for the better part of a day.

Deb and I went on the same trip, yet we captured two different perspectives. I liken it to when you meet someone with a severely scarred face. At first, you only see the scars, but after a while, you fall so in love with the person, you no longer "look at the outward appearance." You begin to see what the Lord looks at—the "heart!"

I don't look at my pictures and see them as somehow missing the point, or too fleshy a perspective. I see them as an exciting beginning of an amazing journey on which the Lord is taking me. He has introduced me to a country and a people with many wounds and many scars. Perhaps, one day, I, too, will no longer notice them, and see only the heart. And, maybe one day those wounds, of a country and of a people, will be healed by the anointing balm of Jesus, This, of course, is for what we, a prayer team, are praying.

Gracious Lord, Thank You for the opportunity to serve You in such a powerful way, through missions. And, thank You for the privilege and the freedom to have a relationship with You so that You might teach us Your Word in real and meaningful ways. You are an awesome God! We love You, amen.

Weekly Wisdom Walk

Read 1 Samuel 16:1–13. *Samuel Anoints David.* Is there a person or circumstance in your life that finds you looking at the "outward appearance" instead of the heart? Pray for the Lord to reveal this to you.

...and the moon became as red as blood (Rev. 6 :12, NLT).

Week 6

RED-ORANGE MOON

Sovereignty

When I saw the Lamb open the sixth seal, I looked and saw a great
earthquake. The sun turned as dark as sackcloth, and the moon became
as red as blood. The stars in the sky fell to earth, just like figs shaken
loose by a windstorm. Then the sky was rolled up like a scroll, and
all mountains and islands were moved from their places. The kings
of the earth, its famous people, and its military leaders hid in caves
or behind rocks on the mountains. They hid there together with the
rich and the powerful and with all the slaves and free people.
—Revelation 6:12–15, CEV

It was a crystal clear mid-summer evening, when I noticed the full moon.
Not the blue moon making its second appearance in a month's time, but
a vibrant red-orange moon, unlike any color I'd ever seen it before. It
was spectacular. I dashed to our highest point, with camera in hand, to take
some pictures and enjoy it. The moon was still low to the ground, no stars yet
visible. It was alone in the sky, a big, fiery red ball against a sea of blackness.
Captivating!

Afterward, I dashed to my Internet browser. What was this anomaly I experienced? To my amazement, the websites to scour for information were plentiful.
The first, a blog, was almost as fascinating to me as the incredible splendor in
the sky I had witnessed. For those who read, write, or visit blogs, the format
and the content can range as far and wide as the imagination can span, but not
this one. For more than three years, this blog had been sustained by only one
subject, this red-orange moon, a spectacle, stopping people in their tracks across
the globe for years. As it turns out, there is a perfectly scientific reason for the

phenomenon. The sun, Earth, and moon are all in alignment, and the Earth's atmosphere filters out the blue in the spectrum, making our eye see more of the red. Yet, what was remarkable to me is how these singular episodes, caught at various moments, globally tethered an entire world together, one person at a time. Each blogger posted their heart's response to the visual. Many mentioned God's greatness. Someone started this blog, and in their own way, were going out, via cyberspace, and "making disciples of all nations" (Matt. 28:19).

It's incredible how we travel the Internet superhighway and become connected with people in an instant. In this age of e-mail, instant messaging, Twitter, Skype, and text messaging, we can be halfway around the world in a blink of an eye. How long did it take Paul's epistles to travel to his intended audiences by camel, donkey, rat-infested ships, on foot, and via unsafe roads riddled with bandits and prey? What took weeks or months for Paul, takes us less than a second today. And, he (or someone on his behalf, rather) wrote his letters the "old fashioned" way, on a scroll with no spell check.

In Revelation, John tells of his vision as the sixth seal is opened and the moon turns blood red. Certainly, John refers to much chaos and confusion in his spiritual vision. There was a certain amount of confusion in each of the posts I read, as well. One, in particular, thought at first it might be "end times" as John describes. John also speaks of pandemonium, kings, the wealthy as well as the poor, literally, everyone, no matter their social stature, all coming together and running and hiding in the caves and under the rocks, as if this is not a time for hierarchy. Those of us visiting the blog didn't know whether we were in the presence of royalty or paupers, either. We were just drawn to something bigger than all of us. When will we stop allowing calamity or anonymity to be the things that tear down the walls of class structure and simply come together as people of God?

After considering all the parallels, I wondered, what might these end times look like to us when Jesus comes again? John's apocalyptic vision uses ancient terminology. Fast forward. What will it sound like, when we all drop our laptops and turn off our cell phones? Or, will we take a moment to send a quick text message? Will all the home and car alarms go off at once from the thunderous earthquake? Will we even hear them over the rapture, and where will we run? And, why? As the Psalmist says:

> Where can I go from your Spirit? Where can I flee from your presence? If I go up to the heavens, you are there; if I make my bed in the depths, you are there. If I rise on the wings of the dawn, if I settle on the far side of the sea, even there your hand will guide me;

your right hand will hold me fast. If I say, "Surely the darkness will hide me and the light become night around me," even the darkness will not be dark to you; the night will shine like the day, for darkness is as light to you.

—PSALM 139:7–12

God of the Universe, You are all-knowing and all-seeing. We honor You for never giving up on us, when we fall away and hide. Thank You for pursuing Your children and for connecting us in ways, which reminds us You are ever-present, in times of turmoil as well as times of knee dropping awe! We revel in Your splendor. Draw us nearer to You and to each other, Dear Jesus. Let us decrease, so that You might increase. In Your name we pray, amen

WEEKLY WISDOM WALK

Do you ever have those "small-world" moments? You know the ones when the world gets a lot smaller through something connects us all. Isn't it nice to know we are woven into a massive fabric by God's design? We are but a tiny strand in it. Does this make you feel insignificant and small or help you recognize just how mighty and enormous our God truly is? We cannot escape Him. He is sovereign over not just our lives, but over everything, everyone, and all of creation. He is the God of the universe. That also means we are fully known by God, so there is no point in escaping Him. He knows our thoughts and our actions, even those not acted upon. Spend some time in praise and prayer this week about God's sovereignty over your life, and ask yourself two questions: If God could send you a text message, right now, what might it say? And, what if you could send one to God, right this instant, what would *you* say? I love You? BRB (Be Right Back)? If that was your first thought, talk to Him about it. No condemnation, remember? "Therefore, there is now no condemnation for those who are in Christ Jesus" (Rom. 8:1). God wants you to come to Him with all of it, authentically. He is closer than a text message away!

Give ear and come to me; Listen, that your soul may live (Isa. 55:3).

SILENT WATERFALL

Busyness

Give ear and come to me; Listen, that your soul may live.
—ISAIAH 55:3

I REMEMBER WHEN WE first installed our backyard waterfall, transforming a forty- or fifty-foot dirt hill into a master workmanship that was intended to carry us away from our day-to-day troubles into deep communion with God's creation. It was so majestic, tall, and overwhelming and... well, once we cranked it up... loud, my husband offered! "Loud?!" I retorted, in utter confusion. The sound of water, so serene, diverging off of, literally, tons of rocks, cascading into a pool of water, rippling, and recycling and doing it all again and again? Perpetual motion of a different sort than our busy lives, calling us, beckoning us to come and sit, to come and just be. I suppose it took some getting used to for my husband, but not very long. One afternoon by the water, and all of a day's cares could instantly be washed away. The sound was meditative.

When spring ushered in, the flowers planted on the hill burst to greet us with vibrant color. Bird feeders and birdhouses were added. In the cool of the night, we could sleep with the windows open and allow the sound of the water to lull us to sleep like God's very own lullaby. By day, our sanctuary became a silent retreat in the midst of a busy city and a busy lifestyle. The songs of the birds, the rustling of the trees, the scampering of the squirrels and the symphonic sounds of the waterfall only served to remind us that we had found "real" silence and solitude, for it is when we *stop* hearing nature's music, that we realize we have exchanged silence for noise—the noise of our culture, be it traffic, media, or simply the noise in our heads.

But, we do get caught up in our busyness and our worldliness, don't we? This point was driven home recently with me, when I realized I couldn't remember the last time I actually "heard" my waterfall. "Who silenced my waterfall?" I thought. I cracked the upstairs window. I heard nothing. I looked out another window from upstairs, and though I could see it running, still, I heard nothing. When did this happen? When did my busyness replace my need, the command, to be still? *"Be still and know that I am God"*(Ps. 46:10). How much noise must have built up, over how long a period of time, to completely obliterate what was at first perceived to be *loud*?

God invites us to lean in, incline our ear toward Him… "Give ear and come to me; listen, that you may live" (Isa. 55:3). It is this deep, abiding communion with our Lord and Savior that I had once experienced by the waterfall. Somewhere along the way, I fell back into the snare of this world. Don't we all do that from time to time? We somehow start doing all of the talking and stop listening. Words and noise fill up our days, and before we know it, we have not only drowned out the bird songs, but we can no longer hear the Divine whispers of the One who gave us the words in the first place. And, the waterfall falls in silence.

> *Gracious and loving Lord, when I am distracted by the flesh and things of this world, when spiritual warfare turns my attention away from You, send me a birdsong I might hear. Let the waterfalls of my life continue to cascade melodiously, reminding me of Your omni-presence showering over me and beckoning me to take time to draw nearer to You. Let there not be a season of my life where we are apart. I want to incline my ear toward You always, and listen, so that I may live. In Jesus' precious and Holy name, amen*

Weekly Wisdom Walk

Do you have a special place where you experience utter silence? Where all you hear is the sounds of God's creation? If so, make an appointment on your calendar to spend some quality time there this week. If not, carve out some time to simply be alone. Bring a Bible, and read 1 Kings 19:11–12. God does not always present himself in spectacular ways. We do not need to search for a burning bush. Just stop, and be. Listen. Be still. Pray to hear God's divine breathings to your heart—the still, small voice.

Elizabeth Barrett Browning wrote in her *Aurora Leigh*:

Earth's crammed with heaven And every common bush afire with God:
But only he who sees, takes off his shoes, The rest sit round it, and pluck
   blackberries.

Take off your shoes. You are on Holy ground. This is a time for you to be
authentic and deeply personal with your Father in Heaven, Who wants an
intimate relationship with you. Spend this time in connection, or re-connec-
tion, with Him. Pray out loud, if it is helpful for you. This is between you and
your Father. Enjoy your time together. Lift high, your burdens, to the One who
created the towering, melodious waterfalls of your life, and let them become
audible once again—a trickle at first, maybe, then, a flood of wonder washing
away all of the unnecessary noise that distracted you from our utmost and
most High.

Jesus wept (John 11:35).

TEARS FROM HEAVEN

Brokenness

Jesus wept.
—JOHN 11:35

SITTING IN THE doctor's office, waiting to see whether the results of their tests revealed a positive result for breast cancer, my mother met the woman who soon became her best friend. Though Maria's test results were benign, it did not stop her from battling this disease with my mother, whose results were not benign. Maria had tremendous compassion for the suffering world. I remember whenever we would drive past someone's dead pet alongside the road; she would utter, with a heartfelt sadness, "Tears will be shed today." If we passed a funeral procession, she whispered a prayer. When passing a cemetery, she would silence the radio out of respect for the mourners. I was drawn to the dignity of this woman and wanted to emulate the morality and honor she effortlessly exemplified.

A few years later, my mother lost her battle with cancer, and I found myself turning off the radio before I entered the iron gates of the national cemetery to place yellow roses, a family favorite, at her gravesite. More than three decades later, I still follow this ritual. This week, as my son and I passed a funeral procession, I explained to him about "drive by" prayers and having more than just a passing connection with those around you. I explained to him why I turn the radio off and sundry other things I do.

I have always had a heart for the wounded—born of my own wounds, perhaps, but I imagine my mother's dear friend planted a seed. This, on some level, is why I ultimately felt called to missions, I think. There are so many forms of missions, from mending walls to mending hearts. I've come to realize, every country, including our own, needs them all. Yet, I am drawn to the wounds of the heart. In our suffering world, we are not lacking of hearts aching to be held by the nail-scarred palms of Jesus.

Whether their ache comes from extreme poverty, death, grief, loss, substance abuse, physical or mental illness, dysfunction, the failure of a government, recovery from the aftermath of war... whatever. We are a fallen world. And, Jesus knew it. That is why He came. He came to take away the sins of the world, but He did it in the most human and godly way possible. He did it with feeling. His entire journey to the cross was both divine and human. He felt what we feel, especially when it came to the suffering of the world.

The shortest verse in the Bible is found in John, Chapter 11:35, "Jesus wept." No more words are necessary to capture all that is said in this simple scripture. It speaks of a Lord who cares, one who has compassion and empathy. It tells us Jesus is unafraid to express His emotions openly. He does not suppress them. He is authentic.

While walking around a town in Bosnia after a hard rain, I was captivated by the reminders of war visually scarring the surface of many of the buildings. However, below the surface in these passionate people there was a battle still raging. The war has been over for fifteen years, but deep inside, at the heart level, there is a battle being waged for their joy and their hope. Those who have found Jesus are holding on with a white-knuckled grip to His nail-scarred hands. Those who do not know Him, walk the streets of this town, with no industry, aimlessly, with little delight in each step, nowhere to go, nothing to look forward to, no hope for a future.

As I passed yet another storefront building marred from shelling and never repaired for lack of funds to do so, I noticed a single yellow rose—our family favorite. It was drizzled with raindrops. Tears from Heaven, I think, for "*Jesus wept*" (John 11:35). Just as He wept for Lazarus, Mary, and Martha, He weeps for a country. He weeps for His people. He weeps for you and me.

Precious Father, thank You for creating us in Your own image and, then, sending Your Son in ours, fully human. Thank You for Your desire to want a relationship with us, for the price You paid to know our suffering and then taking on the sins of a broken world. Help us to love as You love and to have a heart for the wounded. Help us to live our lives as Your Son, Jesus, did, with compassion and feeling. In His name we pray, amen.

Weekly Wisdom Walk

Is it difficult for you to think of Jesus as totally human? We imagine an angelic birth with a heavenly light, but as sure as there were cows in the stable, there was manure as well. Blistering summer heat in the desert, most certainly had our Savior, a carpenter, breaking a sweat. Sound irreverent? He was very much human. We count on His humanity. It is how we are fully known. It is by God's design. Read John Chapter 11, the story of Lazarus' death. Dig deeper into the very nature of Jesus and His humanness. Try to connect with your Lord and Savior in prayer on a very intimate level this week.

See, I am doing a new thing! Now it springs up; do you not perceive it? I am making a way in the desert (Isa. 43:19).

OASIS

Temptation

Forget the former things; do not dwell on the past. See, I am
doing a new thing! Now it springs up; do you not perceive it? I
am making a way in the desert and streams in the wasteland.
—ISAIAH 43:18–19

I REMEMBER THE FIRST time I learned the word, mirage. We were driving to California from Texas on a long stretch of highway, nothing but straight, black roadway dead ahead, sand-filled desert to either side. Nothing to gaze upon either, save for the wisps of tumbleweed crisscrossing the highway aimlessly and hopelessly lost. Gazing at the asphalt in the distance, the road appeared wet or, as we Texans might be quick to assume, slick with oil. My parents explained it was only a mirage. "What is a mirage?" I asked. I was told it is like an oasis. But unlike an oasis, it is not really there. Your eyes deceive you, and your mind allows it.

Sure enough, as soon as our car would reach the mirage, it was simply more of the same road traveled.

The whole scene reminds me of the desert traveler depicted in Hollywood films, escaping his captors, looking to reunite with allies, then, finally giving up hope and settling simply for survival instead. Just a trickle of water from a cactus would do.

Sometimes, we get a peek into his thoughts—everything he will do right from now on, just for a little bit of water, a little mercy. Or flashes back on the past and all that went wrong leading up to this point in time. How did he... indeed, how did *we*, get to this place?

It is an age-old question? The Israelites asked themselves the same question on more than one occasion, and every time, God delivered them from their misery. The Israelites made a habit of dwelling on the past and not letting things go. Do you ever do that? Find yourself on more of the same road traveled? I do. And, for me, it tends to perpetuate the very misery from which God has delivered me!

It is in those times, I am the man in the desert no longer hoping to find a friendly ally to come rescue me. I will be content to find a pool of water to quench my thirst. I must take great care to avoid temptation and not seek out the mirage, but the oasis. Not to allow my eyes or my mind to deceive me, because the evil one stands ready to pounce at my willingness to settle for less. "Keep a cool head. Stay alert. The Devil is poised to pounce, and would like nothing better than to catch you napping. Keep your guard up. You're not the only ones plunged into these hard times. It's the same with Christians all over the world. So keep a firm grip on the faith. The suffering won't last forever" (1 Peter 5:8–9, The Message).

This is not a physical thirst I suffer, but a spiritual thirst for Jesus, my living water, real oasis water! It is a thirst for His mercy and His presence. No longer feeling alone in the desert of my life, not knowing how I got there, but thrilled I broke free of what held me captive and separated from Him, I am desperately running, perhaps aimlessly, though still seeking to find the only One to whom I can surrender these thoughts of things past—the shame, the anger, the bitterness, the brokenness, the sadness. He is ready to take it all. I know I can release these destructive patterns and ways of thinking and set my eyes and my mind on Him. The mirages will disappear and in their place will be glory. I will be reminded of the words of the prophet Isaiah, "Forget the former things; do not dwell on the past. See, I am doing a new thing! Now it springs up; do you not perceive it? I am making a way in the desert and streams in the wasteland" (Isa. 43:18–19). And, I will be refreshed and replenished in the pool of God's mercy.

> *Gracious God, You are a merciful Father and we love You. Thank You for Your faithfulness to us and forgive us for our unfaithfulness. Help us to be mindful of our thoughts and our actions. When we dwell on the past, remind us of our future with You. Teach us to avoid the mirages of life and the temptations of a quick fix. When we find ourselves in the deserts, remind us to hold faithfully to the truth that Your oasis is near. In Your precious Son Jesus' name, amen.*

Weekly Wisdom Walk

Dwelling on the past! Who hasn't done this? Spend some time this week thinking about the last time you set your mind on "former things." Did it make you feel any better? Maybe it is something on your mind right now. Did you go for the mirage—a little "harmless" gossip to make you feel better perhaps—or were you able to find the oasis offered in our Lord Jesus? In Philippians 4:8, Paul offers a paradigm shift for our thought world, "Finally, brothers and sisters, whatever is true, whatever is noble, whatever is right, whatever is pure, whatever is lovely, whatever is admirable—if anything is excellent or praiseworthy—think about such things." In 2 Corinthians 10:5, he offers another one, "We demolish arguments and every pretension that sets itself up against the knowledge of God, and we take captive every thought to make it obedient to Christ." Place these scriptures in conspicuous places in your home where you might notice them this week. The next time you find yourself dwelling on the past, try putting them into practice.

Weeping may endure for a night, but joy comes in the morning (Ps. 30:5, NKJV).

Week 10

WEEPING WILLOW

The Enemy

Weeping may endure for a night, but joy comes in the morning.
—Psalm 30:5, nkjv

Have you ever thought about how many clichés are rooted in scripture?

- **"I can see the writing on the wall"** speaks of Daniel's ability to interpret for King Belshazzar, "Suddenly the fingers of a human hand appeared and wrote on the plaster of the wall, near the lampstand in the royal palace. The king watched the hand as it wrote" (Dan. 5:5).

- **"Don't go to bed angry"** recalls Mosaic law where you may be justified in your anger, but bitterness is a whole other story. Nothing should be stewed on and simmered overnight. "Do not let the sun go down while you are still angry" (Eph. 4:26).

- **"Everything will look better in the morning"** references a renewed perspective as seen through the eyes of the Psalmist, when darkness fades and light, restored. "Weeping may endure for a night, but joy comes in the morning" (Ps. 30:5, nkjv).

I don't believe we realize the depth of meaning in these verses when we paraphrase them in cliché. Over time, "Everything will look better in the morning" has become quite literal—a problem more easily manageable once we sleep on it. We've lost the magnitude of the darkness and light metaphor of which the psalmist speaks. Our haughtiness and self-righteous belief that we can go it alone separates us from the One through whom nothing is impossible. This thought is insidious and deceptive, seeping in when we least expect it and, like a virus, quickly overcomes us. Too often, it is subconscious—something we say or do. It is an action, not a thought at all, and the path to darkness, to night, is being paved while we are left unawares.

Maybe we have spoken harshly in response to being mistreated. We feel justified in our anger. We never saw this coming but, now, we "see the writing on the wall" and it is indelibly clear. Guilty! The object of our wrath is a deserving recipient. Their treatment of us was unfair. Our response, one of self-preservation and self-defense was not emotional, just on-point, accurate, well placed. Why doesn't it feel right later, or the next day? Maybe a week goes by, a month, years. This is the darkness, at least one example. Indeed we went to bed angry. We stewed, grew bitter. Anger turns to rage and surely weeping will follow. We are deeply anguished. How did we get here? So far away from the only One who can heal us from our affliction and bring us out of the darkness into the morning light.

One of my mother's favorite trees was the Weeping Willow. She did not live long enough to see it "weep." What a sad name for a beautiful tree. One could say it is named for its drooping branches, but I like to think of them as bowing down. Like those of us who discover we have been walking in darkness by our own choosing, only to realize the way back to our Lord and Savior is through an act of knee-dropping confession. Reorienting our life, placing the Lord first, choosing forgiveness, grace, even when we are wronged or persecuted, seeking God's counsel instead of our own—these actions will lead to the repentance we need and the joy that comes in the morning. The morning is the light. The light, Jesus. Darkness doesn't only last a night. It can last a lifetime, yet so can the morning—the light. It is your choice. We are all one choice away from seeing the Willow as weeping or bowing.

> *Loving Lord, we praise You for being a forgiving and gracious God who waits for us and pursues us even when we turn away. Thank You for Your incredible faithfulness and patience. Thank You for Your tremendous sacrifice so that we may ask Your forgiveness and be restored, renewed, and redeemed. Help us, Lord, to make wise choices. When we are quick to respond and when that response doesn't feel right, remind us of the Willow Tree. Let us bow rather than weep. In Your name we pray, amen!*

Weekly Wisdom Walk

Have you made any choices lately that just don't feel like your "finest hour?" Is there any unrest in you, which might be traced back to a choice in which you could have sought godly counsel first? Sometimes, we don't feel like we have anything to repent, but upon deeper, Christ-oriented, examination, something percolates to the surface and God reveals an area of our lives that was not surrendered to Him. Once exposed, we have opened up the way to repentance and the healing balm of our Lord Jesus. In *The Message*, Psalm 139:23–24 says, "Investigate my life, O God, find out everything about me; Cross-examine and test me, get a clear picture of what I'm about; See for yourself whether I've done anything wrong—then guide me on the road to eternal life." Pray this scripture back to God this week and see if there is a Weeping Willow in your life, weary of weeping and ready to bow.

"Sir, give me this water so that I won't get thirsty and have to keep coming here to draw water" (John 4:15).

LIVING WATER

New Life

Jesus answered, "Everyone who drinks this water will be thirsty again,
but whoever drinks the water I give him will never thirst. Indeed, the
water I give him will become in him a spring of water welling up to
eternal life." The woman said to him, "Sir, give me this water so that
I won't get thirsty and have to keep coming here to draw water."
—JOHN 4:13–15

ONE YEAR, FOR spring break, my husband, son and I returned to my
hometown for a visit. It had been eight years since they had been
back, only a few for me. It is always a difficult journey home for me,
I must admit. Fond memories interwoven with many tragic ones always seem
to await me. Much of my years of brokenness before finding the light of Jesus
began there and many of the reminders, standing as icons of that brokenness
still remain today, more than three decades later.

Each trip, I make my annual pilgrimage to many of these symbolic places—
the home where I grew up, my parents' gravesite, and others—to pay homage
to a past with which I have made peace and from which I have been delivered.
By the grace of God and the anointing balm of forgiveness, there has long since
been healing and restoration. Yet, as many healing stories go... "it is a journey
not a destination." There is something about this "returning," which makes me
lose sight of the Holy Spirit I now have within, guiding me. I become again,
flesh. Like the Samaritan woman at the well, I return with a non-spiritual
perspective, drawing, through hard labor, from a well that will never quench
my thirst.

All of this came clear to me as I started to view my hometown through the innocent eyes of my then pre-teenaged son. Having been too young to remember his last visit, he seemed to be appreciating this exciting city for the first time. These somber icons were filled with amazing new revelations for me, through the eyes of a child. He noticed things I had never before seen. And, soon, I understood why. He had no ties to my past. He never knew his grand-parents. He was not jaded by circumstances. This place was quite simply new, uncharted territory.

On the last day of our visit, we took a long hike in the country, into what also seemed "uncharted territory." We went by caravan. My brother and I led the way. I rode on the back of his motorcycle, while our spouses, children and sundry other family members followed in cars. On the ride, I had over an hour to reflect on this very different week we had experienced. We took in new sights and played every bit the tourist for the first time in our years of travel there. Yet, for more than thirty-five years, I found myself, at one time, or another, on the back of my brother's motorcycle. Never once, did we entertain the notion, in the midst of our chaotic childhoods, there would come a time when we'd be middle-aged, still riding, with our families in tow. I was holding on to my brother, but it occurred to me that there was no longer any need to hold on to the rest of it; the troubling symbols and icons. They had to be let go—right down to the chain I still wore around my neck, which was becoming more and more, a noose.

I do not want to be like the Samaritan woman before she met Jesus at the well. I want to be like her afterward! The woman said to Him, "Sir, give me this water so that I won't get thirsty and have to keep coming here to draw water" (John 4:15). Sometimes, I think even we, as Christians, need a reminder to continue to drink the living water, so we don't thirst. We have all we need in Jesus. Everything else has been taken care of.

On our hike, my son delighted in the bodies of water fed by the many springs that bubble up to the surface, creating crystal-clear streams, creek beds, and rivers for skipping stones. With the Spirit-led fervor of Christ from within, my son threw himself into every spring-fed stream and bathed himself in the cool water throughout our near five-mile trek, while my husband took pictures of the new birth of spring, barely budding on the barren branches above. It was a joy to see them revel in God's creation. At one point, my son gazed at the clear water, then looked up quizzically, and asked, "Can we drink this water?" I wish I had the answer for him then, which I have now.

Gracious heavenly Father, thank You for a well that never runs dry,
for the gift of my child's eyes helping me to see as You see, and for a

*husband, who could capture, on film, the new birth beginning in me
as yet another layer of healing has begun on my journey with You.
Thank You for Your creation, for motorcycle rides, for big brothers,
and for the powerful ways You bring all things together as we come to
Your well to drink. In Jesus' Holy name, amen*

Weekly Wisdom Walk

As Christians, I think we all fall into the trap of returning to the well, as opposed
to remembering we have "living water" from which to draw and quench our
spiritual thirst. Does this ever happen to you? Think about times when you fall
into this trap? Is it a pattern? A certain compartment of your life, perhaps, not
fully surrendered to our Lord and Savior? God doesn't just want some of you
some of the time. He wants all of you all of the time. Spend time in prayer this
week and ask God to reveal areas of your life that are not completely surrendered to Him. If you have wounds that still require healing, pray about those as
well. Expose them, through prayer, to the healing balm of Jesus.

Love your enemies and pray for those who persecute you (Matt. 5:44).

GREATEST MOMENTS

Forgiveness

But I tell you: Love your enemies and pray for those who persecute you.
—MATTHEW 5:44

WHAT IS THE best thing you have ever done in your life? Top three greatest moments. Have you ever been asked this question? I have. As Moms, our knee-jerk answer is to respond with the birth of a child. How can we not? It is a miraculous event. On our crisp school morning commute, my son and I were talking about "things that don't look like they should work" and, although I didn't think about this until now, pregnancy and childbirth are definitely among them in my book. That will always be one of life's miracles to me. It just does not look like it should work—but God safely knits those babies together in a mother's womb and it works! Praise the Lord!

Yes, I would definitely have to say childbirth is in my top three, actually, number three. Still, it is not the best moment, the standout event, or recollection. Baptism? The moment you accepted Jesus as your Lord and Savior? Absolutely, those are huge! Top five, for sure, but not in my top three. Surprised?

I would have to say one of my three would have to be the event that preceded the moment I came to know Jesus as my Lord and Savior. The act that removed my veil (2 Cor. 3:16–18) and caused me to gaze squarely into the eyes of Jesus and know, unequivocally, that He is the Lord of my life. This was a moment of forgiveness. This is the moment when I chose to no longer to be the victim, but instead, the victor. I forgave my father, who abandoned me as a teenager, after my mother died. My father was a man who struggled with alcoholism and was not able to pull himself out of his own downward spiral of grief, in order to care for his own child. Yet, the one who lived with the shackled heart of anger, bitterness, and rage was not him, it was me. My mentor, pastor, counselor and friend, Lex, led me to the cross and opened up the path to forgiveness, modeled by our loving Lord, so that I might be capable of such a selfless act. In doing so, the captive was set free. The veil was removed and the transformation of my heart began. Greatest moment, number two. Do you hear the vinyl record screeching yet? What? Number two?

What could possibly surpass the moment in which one has come to know Jesus as Lord? For me, it is when greatest moment number one and greatest moment two intersect—when I discovered what greatness God had done *in* me, He was now going to do *through* me. Unlike my tragic childhood, my husband and I wanted our son to know Jesus and grow up in the church. More importantly, we needed for him to have a moral compass. We wanted to teach him early about grace, mercy, and forgiveness. My entire life testimony hangs on a moment of forgiveness. As early as preschool, we taught our son, not just to say "I'm sorry" or accept the apologies of others, but to add another step, the "I forgive you." Like all children, he has had his share of bully encounters. This has provided opportunities to teach him God's principles of grace and forgiveness.

As a pre-teen, he became a victim of a cruel prank. Ironically, it occurred just before I was to leave for my mission trip to a war-torn Bosnia, still shackled by un-forgiveness, hatred, persecution, and intolerance. What happened to my son became a microcosm of the elements pervasive in the region to which I was called to minister. We need not go further than our own backyards to practice this concept of forgiveness. It is almost a daily force with which to be reckoned. Yet, because of my life story, God has cultivated in me a heart for the wounded, the least, the lost, both the hater and the hated. My number one greatest moment? It is when I discovered my son has this heart as well. He forgave his persecutors and prayed for them each night. He knows he is called to do what is right, and the only choice is the choice Jesus modeled on the cross—forgiveness.

Precious Lord Jesus, It is with humble hearts that we kneel before the foot of the cross and thank You for Your eternal sacrifice and gracious gift of forgiveness. You have saved an undeserving world of our sin and modeled an act so counterintuitive that we could not otherwise do it, if You had not shown us how. Bless my child, Lord, and all children who are coming to know You, Your forgiveness, and Your sovereignty over their lives. Lead them to the cross, Lord, and let

their light shine so that others may be drawn to it and know You too.
In Your name we pray, amen.

Weekly Wisdom Walk

Talk to a child about forgiveness this week. Pray for those that persecute you and them, together. Model forgiveness, mercy, and grace in relevant ways for your children. Read forgiveness passages in the Bible. They are plentiful! Reread the Easter story in the Gospels (Mark 15–16).

Look, the Lamb of God, who takes away the sin of the world (John 1:29).

LAMB'S EAR

Sacrifice

The next day John saw Jesus coming toward him and said, "Look,
the Lamb of God, who takes away the sin of the world!
—JOHN 1:29

W EEDS! WHO NEEDS them? They are one in a long list of reasons why I am not a gardener. Allergies are another one, but that's another book! The only thing worse than weeds is winter, when absolutely nothing seems to be thriving except the evergreens. However, there is a weed, which originated in the Middle East, and can be found year-round in the south, including our backyard. It is commonly referred to as Lamb's Ear. Once you have felt the velvety smoothness of its leaves, there is no other name more appropriate for this low-growing shrub. It is beautiful, not at all what one would expect from a weed. We leave it there through fall, as plant material loses its luster in winter, as trees, bushes, and bulbs work underground preparing for next season; and in early spring, as we wait for new life to burst forth in vibrant color.

There is not an inch of our hilltop garden unplanted. So, the Lamb's Ear has a purpose in our garden. It is a sacrificial plant. Once spring arrives, it has to be dug out and removed or else it will choke out the intended recipients of the light of spring. How do we know when to remove it? It starts to bloom! While this may seem a curious forewarning, you must see the hideous stalk that emanates from this angelic shrub. Like a protruding yellowed broom handle, some four to five feet high it rises, drawing every eye to it, yet struggling to turn gaze away. What was once so perfect has taken on something grotesque.

As winter draws to a close and spring comes upon us, I find myself studying this plant and realizing how much it reminds me of Jesus and His sacrifice for all of us. Jesus, the Lamb of God, how perfect He was. He was without sin. The Lamb's Ear, how beautiful and perfect it is. It's symmetry. It's color, light green with a hint of fine silver. A treasure. Yet, its life span, as a weed, is short. Like Jesus, it paves the way, so that others may live. The yellow bloom, the stake, conjures up the image of the cross on which Jesus was crucified, taking on the sin of the world. He, who was without sin, sacrificed. The bloom, our sin, too hideous to gaze upon must be removed so beauty can be restored.

To be a gardener, it takes a gentle hand and a loving heart, a heart that loves beyond measure; the heart of a gracious, merciful, and faithful God. I cannot love like this, but I can try. I am thankful, however, for the Lamb's Ear. God has sent me a reminder of Jesus. I see Him all year long. And, each year, out of the Lamb's Ear, around Easter time, the stake—indeed, the cross—rises on the Calvary of my hilltop garden so I will remember what He did for me. What He did for you. What He did for all of us. The Lamb of God.

> *Lamb of God, who takes away the sins of the world, have mercy on us, Your children. Remind us each and every day what You have done for us. When we fall, pick us up and point us back to the cross. Show us our sin and give us tangible ways to remember your sacrifice for it. Lead us to Your merciful feet. Lead us to the cross. In Your name we pray, amen.*

Weekly Wisdom Walk

Read John 1:29–34, "Jesus the Lamb of God." John the Baptist also paved the way. He paved the way for Jesus. He did not know him as the Son of God at first. Perhaps, like a weed, Jesus might have been someone others would have passed right by. However, the Spirit came upon him during baptism, and this was the sign which not only convinced John the Baptist of Jesus as Messiah, but it was the declaration which precipitated the disciples to then follow Jesus. Continue your reading as Jesus calls His disciples to "Follow me." Think about what you would do in that situation? How many weeds do you walk by each day without a second thought? See if you can find a tangible metaphor for your sin or for Jesus that will serve as a reminder of His sacrifice, something that you can return to every time you need to remember what He has done.

Spring/Summer

I am the vine; you are the branches (John 15:5).

SOUR GRAPES

Pruning

I am the vine; you are the branches. If a man remains in me and I in
him, he will bear much fruit; apart from me you can do nothing.
—JOHN 15:5

OR AS LONG as I can remember, I have been a leader. As far back as
my youth, I would rise up as the organizer of childhood games. I am a
visionary and a dreamer. However, as much as this has been one of my
strengths, it has also been my Achilles' heel. Even if the occasion doesn't call
for it, I will find myself bubbling to the surface as the leader. Often this has
put me in situations where I find myself in over my head—overwhelmed and
overloaded. Why? My cup will soon overflow with responsibility and, instead
of going to God; I begin to rely on my own strength instead of His power.

I'm also considered a worthy team player. Better, of course, if I am leading
it. But, there again, I can get myself into trouble. I think I am beginning to
learn that I can either lead or I can grow. I can't seem to do both. Inasmuch as
I am a multi-tasker, these are simply two that don't mix with me. Like oil and
vinegar, they're a great combination, but it takes a lot of work to keep them
from following separate paths. I will get so caught up in the responsibility of
leading and the growth of those I'm entrusted to lead, that my own growth
suffers.

It is then that I cry out to my Lord and Savior, "I never wanted this responsibility in the first place, Lord. I can't be everything to everybody!" Like the
Fox in Aesop's fable, "…sour grapes"! I soon realize how ridiculous I sound
and more importantly, that God sees through my feeble attempt to rationalize
the truth. What is needed is a heartfelt, authentic confession. "I've done it

again, Lord. I've allowed my pride to fool me into believing I didn't need You, when apart from You I can do nothing." I don't really expect a vine is going to fall down from the sky and I will swing clear of my predicament, Jane to His Tarzan. I do believe He is sovereign and, given to Him, He will guide my steps away from the mess I created until they glorify Him. "In his heart a man plans his course, but the LORD determines his steps" (Prov. 16:9). This seldom comes without a little pain, mental anguish, or at a minimum, a nice slice of humble pie. This is when I believe God decides it is time for a little pruning.

A recent encounter with this came as part of a group dynamic. The group already had a leader, so the pressure was off. My prayer during this experience was simple," He must increase, but I must decrease" (John 3:30, NKJV). Little did I know how powerfully God would answer me.

In the days that followed my simple prayer, it was unbelievable how many ways my Lord placed me in subservient situations—physically, emotionally, and strategically. I was feeling a little dismissed, left out, left behind. At first, I wasn't connecting the dots. I began to journal some prayers to God each evening. After re-reading them, I once again picked up the pattern. Again, I sounded like sour grapes. Things were not going my way.

As a leader, I am often a focal point, a commanding presence. This was not my experience. I wasn't sure how to follow. I only knew how to lead. Yet, Jesus said, "If anyone wants to be first, he must be the very last, and the servant of all" (Mark 9:35). In this forum, I was enlisted to follow, and God was pruning me to do so. I believe He was teaching me, while I could lead, that did not always mean I should lead. And, more importantly, there are many ways *to* lead!

On the final day of our project, a beautiful backyard vineyard captivated me. The scripture from John came to my mind, "I am the vine; you are the branches. If a man remains in me and I in him, he will bear much fruit; apart from me you can do nothing" (John 15:5). I loved the gnarled branches and how the light shone through the canopy of leaves with the crystal blue sky peeking between the shoots above. Someone had done a wonderful job pruning this vine during the winter. In fact, it left this particular section in the shape of a crooked cross. The poetry of it drew me closer. It was late April and the tiny fruit was beginning to spring forth.

As I continue to look back at this gnarled vine, I can see now how God began this season of pruning in me. "He cuts off every branch in me that bears no fruit, while every branch that does bear fruit he prunes so that it will be even more fruitful" (John 15:2). Today, I find myself leading less, following, surrendering, and listening more and so far, the fruit is denser and sweeter. It has been a challenging season, but sometimes, pruning is painful. I imagine that is what the vine would say, if it could speak.

> *Heavenly Father, You are a patient God. How many times do I lift up the same issues to You in prayer? How many times, Lord, do I make the same mistakes and fall into the same traps? Thank You for Your forgiveness, Your mercy, and Your grace. Thank You for delighting in me, even when I fall and for opening Your arms wide to catch me when I do. Thank You for Your correction, for the loving way You prune me to be better—transformed—into Your likeness. In Jesus' precious and Holy name, I pray. Amen.*

Weekly Wisdom Walk

Read John 15:1–17. What else does John say about our relationship to God in reference to love, joy and friendship? Spend some time digging deep in the passage this week. Ask the Lord to reveal to you any areas in your life right now that need pruning. Or, are there areas you believe are being pruned which you may not have attributed to God's hand? Spend some time in reflection, journaling, and prayer about whatever God places on your heart regarding the vine and the branches. Place a picture of a grapevine on your refrigerator. Commit John 15:5 to memory each time you notice it!

He maketh my feet like hinds' feet, and setteth me upon my high places (Ps. 18:33, KJV).

1062 STEPS

Pride

He maketh my feet like hinds' feet, and setteth me upon my high places.
—PSALM 18:33, KJV

ARE YOU A "read all the instructions first" type person, or do you like to just dive in and figure things out as you go along? I have usually fallen into the latter group. I like to size up the scope of the task and decide if I think I can do it myself, first, and forego the extra time and energy of reading and following instructions. I tell myself I will get to the end result quicker and achieve my goals just the same, without this often-unnecessary formality.

The problem is this doesn't always work. In fact, it rarely works. However, the times I have been victorious without outside help have somehow lured me into a false sense of security. I've also exaggerated the statistics and stacked them in my favor over the years, thinking I'm far more successful at the "do-it-yourself" approach than a good reality check would reflect. As a result, I continue to fall in this trap.

My husband is exactly the opposite. He reads every instruction before he starts anything, making many tasks an all-day project. I don't need to offer up details from a twenty-year marriage to illustrate how this plays out when we purchase something new with seven thousand parts, for example. It's the stuff that makes for any good stand-up comic routine.

The only time this dynamic gets us into any kind of trouble is when we are undertaking the task together. One wants to follow instructions, the other does not. Now, we are at a crossroads, and neither winds up enjoying the journey.

It was spring, and my husband, my son, and I decided to go for a hike at an area state park, complete with waterfalls, incredible foliage in full bloom—the whole picture-perfect setting. I brought my camera, my son hunted for a good walking stick, and my husband, the outdoorsman, well versed in everything that speaks "nature," was just happy to be outside. We got our map of trails (already more information than I needed) and headed for the path. My son and I went charging ahead, while my husband kept this nice, even, steady pace behind us. I was snapping pictures, not really noticing the main events along the path. My son was doing his own thing, and bringing up the rear was my husband.

After a few turns and some pictures in front of waterfalls, we came to a high place atop the ridge, which marked the beginning of the descent down into the valley. There was a sign indicating health warnings as the 1,062 steps, round-trip, were difficult for those with certain medical conditions. No problem. Again, I forged ahead. "Slow down, Babe! Take your time. You're going to want to pace yourself," my husband offered. But, I didn't listen. I didn't feel I needed any instructions to walk down some steps. In fact, I had read more than usual. We didn't have any of those medical conditions, so let's just do this thing and get to the splendor! Not once did I consider my husband had run a marathon, hiked the Georgia mountains on more than one occasion, including a portion of the Appalachian Trail. This would have been an ideal time to think of God's instruction through the wisdom of Solomon, "The way of a fool seems right to him, but a wise man listens to advice" (Prov. 12:15).

When we got to the bottom, it was indeed, breathtaking, but I learned something valuable in the process. It's not going up that's the hard part, as it might seem—it's going down! There is exponentially more pressure on your joints (including my bad knees) on the descent rather than the ascent. By the time we made it to the splendor, I felt less than splendid. In fact, I was less fascinated by what we had come to enjoy and more obsessed with what I was now facing. It was all I could do not to look up at those steps and wonder how in the world I was going to get back up to the high places. In Psalms 18:33, David says, "He maketh my feet like hinds' feet, and setteth me upon my high places." Oh, how I wanted my Lord to simply setteth me back on the ridge up top, or at least, give me the feet, agility, and spring-like quickness of a mountain deer, so I could blink and end the agony I was facing. But, somehow, I didn't believe this was my plight.

I did not listen to my husband, wise and experienced, in the same way I do not always follow the Word of God. Pride allows me to fall away and deceive myself into believing I can handle things of my own power and strength, despite the fact that God has given me the best instruction manual there is—His Word! This is the manual for living under His authority. But remaining in the Word requires discipline. I imagine a similar discipline as reading instructions might require. I may be able to survive without knowing how to put together my latest purchase without instructions, but when it comes to living my life?

Merciful Father, Your grace is as boundless as Your creation. There is nowhere we can go to escape it. Thank You for Your great love and Your faithfulness, even when we are disobedient, undisciplined, or inattentive. Grant us Your mercy when we fall astray and draw us back to You. Help us to make time to revel in Your Word and to hide these treasures in our heart as instructions to live by. In Your son's precious and Holy name, amen.

WEEKLY WISDOM WALK

God wants to lead us out of the valleys of life and return us to the mountaintops with renewed strength, agility, and sure footedness, but He wants us to get there with the character of Jesus, led by the Sprit within us. His Word is the instruction manual—the word map—to the destination we seek. Psalms 119:11 says, "I have hidden your word in my heart that I might not sin against you." Spend some time this week doing just that—hiding God's Word in your heart. He delights in you. Delight in Him and His words to you. Proverbs and Psalms are great places to start if you are new to reading the Bible and just want to read some "poetry." In fact, if you read one Proverb and one Psalm a day, corresponding to the day of the week, plus every thirtieth Psalm after that (a total of five Psalms and one Proverb each day), you will have read the entire books of Psalms and Proverbs in a 31-day calendar month. (For example, on the fifth day of the month, read Proverbs 5, and Psalms 5, 35, 65, 95, and 125).

Stretch out your hand toward the sky so that darkness will spread over Egypt — darkness that can be felt (Exod. 10:21).

ASH RAIN

Self-Involvement

Then the LORD said to Moses, "Stretch out your hand toward the sky
so that darkness will spread over Egypt—darkness that can be felt."
—EXODUS 10:21

I T WAS MARCH, and after a long day of playing tourist in my home state
of Texas, it began to rain. We pulled over in front of our hotel so my son
could switch cars. He was going to spend the night with relatives. I hopped
out at the curb and ran to my family's vehicle behind us. We decided to run
inside the hotel first and grab a few overnight supplies for him. As I leaned in
to speak through the car window, I could feel the rain pressing between the
palms of my hands and the passenger side door of their car. I spoke quickly,
annoyed by the inconvenience of wet hair, only slightly registering the rain
felt... shall I say...not like rain. It was grainy. It wasn't cool or refreshing. It was
unusual.

But, I had an agenda. There were cars jockeying for position. Drivers pleading
with their facial expressions for our primo spots. The rain was increasing and
it was beginning to look ominous. It was getting darker by the minute. There
was no time for rain analysis. I was on a mission. We had to make a quick
exchange. Everybody in. Grab some necessities. Everybody out. That was the
plan. The drill worked to perfection.

Later we learned more about the peculiar rain. It seems there was a massive
dust storm, brush fire, or both (I believe the jury is still out on that one) in
northern Mexico—Keep in mind we're in central Texas! The winds had carried
soot, dust, dirt, and sand all the way to our destination, sprinkling it across the
lower half of Texas. The cars were covered, bumper-to-bumper, with what looked

like specks of ash. Every carwash in south Texas enjoyed record patronage the following day. The newspapers and blogs were buzzing with commentaries on the oddity in the region's weather. Science experts and environmentalists were analyzing the foreign substance.

But, where was I on the subject, just the night before, when I barely registered an unsettling difference to the sensation of the rain on my palms? I was in denial! At the risk of beating an old cliché, "It's not just a river in Egypt!" But, it was in Egypt when Pharaoh was also in deep denial that the Lord of Israel was who Moses claimed. By the ninth plague, you would think Pharaoh would have relented, but he did not. He also had his own agenda. So, the Lord spread darkness over Egypt. This was the Khamsin, a sand storm that blows off the Sahara. However, this was no ordinary sand storm. The locusts and the hail had already destroyed all the vegetation. The land was more barren than ever. The storm was so dense and thick; visibility was poor. Even the sun was obscured from view. And, when does this phenomenon occur? In March!

The synergy is unbelievable, but true. There I was with ash, dust, dirt, and sand raining down on me so thick I could feel it coming from the darkening sky. It was just as Scripture reads—darkness that can be felt. What did Pharaoh do? Resist. He was thinking about himself. What did I do? Resist. Could I have taken a second to pause and ask, "What is going on here?" In fact, first reports were the ash was from a volcano eruption. Did I stop to think of possible casualties? Pray for them? Pharaoh's heart was hard, but sometimes my heart is too. My heart is hard when I get too wrapped up in myself and my own plans. My heart is hard when I do not stop long enough to consider the plight of others around me or to acknowledge a natural phenomenon, albeit explainable or not. This rendezvous with family became one of those precious childhood memories for my son. No doubt about it. We will have to repeat that one! Ash rain? I'm not so sure we're going to experience it ever again.

Father God, I place myself at Your merciful feet and ask Your forgiveness when I become self-involved and my eyes and ears are not squarely set on You. Help me to maintain a laser focus on You, Lord. I don't want to miss a moment with You. Help me to pause amidst my many agendas and take notice of Your glory. Speak Your truths into my heart and soften it where it is hard. In Jesus' name, amen

Weekly Wisdom Walk

Read Exodus chapters 5–11 this week, describing the ten plagues of Egypt and the hardening of Pharaoh's heart. Isaiah also referred to the hardened heart in Isaiah 6:10, which Jesus draws comparison to in the Gospels (Matthew 13:13–15 and Mark 8:17–18). Is there an area of your life right now where you need the Lord to soften your heart? Are you resisting God's truth in His Word about something? Pray and ask for the Lord to reveal this to you. It is never too late to have all of your senses re-engaged.

Carry each other's burdens, and in this way you will fulfill the law of Christ (Gal. 6:2).

SPANISH MOSS

Selflessness

Carry each other's burdens, and in this way you will fulfill the law of Christ.
—GALATIANS 6:2

I AM THE YOUNGEST of three; the last, the baby. My brother and my sister had already left home when my mother passed away. It was spring when she died, and before the year was out, my father had left home as well. Within a year, I found myself living on a Texas ranch, taken in by relative strangers, who knew this friend we call Jesus.

I, however, was just a teen—lost, broken, and lonely. I knew of Jesus, but I didn't know Him. Consequently, I spent many hours on the ranch wondering, "Where is God?" not realizing He was there in the hearts of the ranchers who gave me refuge, who opted to overlook teenage angst and instead "carry another's burdens" and fulfill the law of Christ.

The ranch made this forsaken city girl feel the vastness of my emptiness, as I would gaze out upon acres upon acres of seemingly untouched land save for the herd of livestock that grazed there. Whether perching upon an abandoned tractor, once vibrant and necessary to the cycle of harvest or riding a workhorse out to pasture until there was no sign of life, I could always find brushstrokes of nature echoing my own feelings of desolation.

As grave as this might sound, it became the beginning of my journey to Jesus. My emptying started in this place. Much happens when you spend time in silence and solitude, reflecting. I spent a fair share of time observing as well. There was more to watch in such vast country than all the stimulation a city could possibly offer. New birth of baby farm animals; survival off the land;

chores! Each became metaphors for the work God was beginning in me, new life, independent living, a work ethic.

I developed a love of all kinds of animals during my stay. I enjoyed watching their behaviors. There were birds, which perched on top of cattle and pecked at their back's ridding them of unwelcome creatures that might otherwise make them sick. It is a symbiotic relationship. What the bird takes from the cow, feeds it. The cow, in return, does not become ill. I'm not sure how the cow feels about having a bird on its back all the time, but sacrifice is not without its reward.

Now all grown up and living in the South, I recall this similar, although not identical, relationship when I see Spanish Moss. This beautiful air plant needs no soil to grow. It draws its moisture from the air, or sometimes, from the host plant from which it hangs. In the South, you will see it draping like a lovely canopy from Live Oaks, especially, although I don't believe it has a preference. It is independent of the host plant, except for the support it requires. The moss needs the tree for support. But, in this case, the tree doesn't really "need" the moss, although it is a much more spectacular tree with it, than without it.

My time on the ranch was unforgettable. I believe it was there that I began what became a fifteen-year-long journey to Jesus from the cattle guards straight to His heart. Like the cow and the bird, the tree and the Spanish Moss, the family on the ranch chose to live as Paul instructed the Galatians, to "Carry each other's burdens, and in this way you will fulfill the law of Christ" (Gal 6:2).

The day I left the ranch for college, tears were shed. Each of us had been changed by the experience. In Acts 20:35, Paul recalls the words of Jesus, "It is more blessed to give than to receive." It has been my experience this is because the giver winds up receiving the more beautiful gift of love, which came from their humble act, freely given. Like the Spanish Moss gives magnificence to its host, I hope I left behind something beautiful where vast emptiness once had been.

> *Gracious God, It is only by Your merciful heart I found my way home to You, through the leathered and weathered hands of strangers turned friends in Christ. You are the Divine Provider, sovereign and loving. Nothing in my life's journey has escaped Your reach. I am forever grateful for the way You have pursued me and provided for me until I was ready to be changed by Your grace. Thank You for Your patience and for Your faithfulness. Help me to always remember*

Your devotion to me and to be a light for You in this broken world
full of wounded people. In Jesus' precious and holy name, amen

Weekly Wisdom Walk

Who has carried your burdens? Who carries them now? Or, are you carrying someone's burdens? This week is about servanthood—service to/for others. There is no question where Jesus stands on this issue. He came to us as a servant. He wants us to respond in kind. In Mark 9:35, Jesus says, "If anyone wants to be first, he must be the very last, and the servant of all." This is just one of the ways we show the love of Jesus, which we are commanded to do through scripture. "A new command I give you: Love one another. As I have loved you, so you must love one another. By this all men will know that you are my disciples, if you love one another" (John 13:34–35). This week thank someone for carrying a burden for you, either in the present or in the past. Pray about it first. How do you want to approach them? Write a letter, make a phone call, send an e-mail, bring flowers or a gift? Also, think about someone you might serve this week in a big way. Pray for the Lord to place an opportunity in your path, which might glorify Him through service!

But whenever anyone turns to the Lord, the veil is taken away (2 Cor. 3:16).

BUTTERFLY

Transformation

> But whenever anyone turns to the Lord, the veil is taken away.
> Now the Lord is the Spirit, and where the Spirit of the Lord is,
> there is freedom. And we, who with unveiled faces all reflect the
> Lord's glory, are being transformed into his likeness with ever-
> increasing glory, which comes from the Lord, who is the Spirit.
> —2 CORINTHIANS 3:16–18

EVERY SPRING, WHEN my son was in preschool, we would order a butterfly kit for him. He enjoys science experiments and this one was every bit as intriguing for his parents. Witnessing a complete life cycle, from egg, to larvae, to pupa, to butterfly is fascinating, although by the time the mail system caught up with us, our eggs were typically larvae, or caterpillars, already. These little guys grew to a fairly enormous size, comparatively, considering their only function in life is to eat—shallow existence, perhaps, but one at which they were quite adept. After a couple of weeks, they would begin the process of spinning their chrysalis.

Each day, we would come home and rush to see if there was any movement inside those tiny cloaked dressing rooms, wishing we could catch a glimpse of the glory behind the veil. For what was fading away in the caterpillar was achieving a renewed radiance in the soon to be emerging butterfly. As days passed, the chrysalis became more transparent and at last we began to see movement and a trace of vibrant transforming life. As the butterflies began to emerge, a red liquid drips from the now transparent veil. Not blood, but remnants of the life left behind—the waste no longer needed for the life being transformed into God's magnificent creation. The butterfly exercises its wings until it's strong enough to fly, and then, at last, it finds freedom to soar anew.

The life cycle of the butterfly is not unlike our new life and glory, which Paul describes in his second letter to the Corinthians. "But whenever anyone turns to the Lord, the veil is taken away. Now the Lord is the Spirit, and where the Spirit of the Lord is, there is freedom. And we, who with unveiled faces all reflect the Lord's glory, are being transformed into his likeness with ever-increasing glory, which comes from the Lord, who is the Spirit" (2 Cor 3:16–18).

The Israelites were unable to see beyond Moses' veil. It masked at first the brilliance of the manifest God, which emanated from his face, but ultimately, like the caterpillar, it covered the fading away of temporary glory. For it is in Jesus that we find our wings. The old falls away. We are no longer bound by law, but by grace. As our veils are lifted, so it is with our hearts and our spirits. We are lifted up in Christ, renewed, resurrected, a new birth, transformed into His likeness, no longer like the old. He shed His red blood for us, we shed our old life, the waste of our past, with no condemnation, in drops of red, blood-like liquid as we pump our wings and rally the strength with which He equips us to be like-minded and witnesses for him—to glorify our God and edify His people.

Butterflies do not have a long life span, and I suppose if we could look at this from God's perspective, our life is but a vapor as well. I am grateful for the butterfly and all that it teaches in such a fraction of my lifetime. I don't believe I look at butterflies the same any longer. Butterflies are you and I, transformed into His likeness. No matter what stage we are at in the process, larvae, pupa, chrysalis or butterfly, this is where we are headed, "with ever-increasing glory, which comes from the Lord, who is the Spirit." And, who cannot gaze upon a beautiful butterfly and not be reminded of our God, our creator?

Gracious God, We praise You for transformation, for the privilege to be fashioned into butterflies of the human variety. Thank You for taking away the sins of the world, by shedding the blood of Jesus on the cross at Calvary, so that we might live and know the glory and freedom of being made new through the covenant brought forth by Jesus. Lift up our veils, Lord Jesus. Keep us from hiding in darkness. Help us to shine brightly for You in this world. Transform us into Your likeness so that we may spread our wings and spread the word of the new covenant. In Your name we pray, amen.

Weekly Wisdom Walk

Read 2 Corinthians, Chapter 3:7–18, "The Glory of the New Covenant." Notice the difference between Moses' veil from the Old Testament, placed to cover his face, and the veil removal referenced in Paul's letter. Think about the significance of this veiling and unveiling, covering the splendor (or fading of it) and exposing it. Cross-reference your reading with that from the Old Testament. (Exodus 34:29–35) Where are you in your walk in conjunction with these passages? Spend some time in prayer with our Lord and Savior this week asking how this applies to where you are in your journey, right now.

Yet, O LORD, you are our Father. We are the clay, you are the potter. We are all the work of your hand (Isa. 64:8).

FLOWER-SHAPED BUTTER

Transformation

Yet, O LORD, you are our Father. We are the clay, you
are the potter; we are all the work of your hand.
—ISAIAH 64:8

IT WAS A beautiful, breezy summer night in Florida, the end to a perfect
vacation with the best of friends. So many new memories were made, so
many old memories remembered. But, on this particular night, perhaps
greater than the sound of the waves crashing on the beach just beyond our
outdoor dinner setting—even more amazing to watch than the black silhou-
etted outlines of each of our dinner guests with faces barely illuminated by the
flickering candles losing their fight with the ocean breeze—was the conversation that took place between our young son and the teenage daughter of our
dearest friend.

Our son is an only child, privately schooled. We are by no means what you
would call, "well to do" but for a boy who is surrounded by many who are, he
may not know the difference. Try as we might to downplay it and incorporate
a proper balance in his life, he is subjected to a fair amount of privilege. It is
a constant challenge to teach him, through conversations, acts of service, and
other charitable activities, that we have been abundantly blessed.

Sometimes, no matter how hard we try, we just cannot teach these life
lessons. But, God speaks through people. He will send a messenger, a teacher
of his own choosing. And, if we are fortunate, if we are listening, if we are
watching, we will get to experience one of those divine moments. That is what
happened at dinner that evening.

The grown-ups were talking when the waiter brought the basket of bread and butter to the table. Once the waiter left, everyone began to pass the basket around. I noticed the teenager staring at the butter. "Flower shaped butter," she exclaimed! "I've never seen butter shaped like a flower before." "Wow, I've ONLY seen butter shaped like flowers," our son replied. He didn't say it in a one-upmanship sort of way. He really said it as if it was his first "Aha" moment. For the first time, I think he actually realized he had never stopped to appreciate the fact that someone took the time to shape his butter. Or, that he was able to experience such a thing at all, when it wasn't everyone's reality.

The whole "there are starving children in Africa" bit was just a little over the top and too intangible for him. This was something he could wrap his mind around and be grateful for. Long after the trip, I noticed him paying attention to any new shapes of butter wondering how much our friend would enjoy them.

Sitting as a captive audience, with the waves crashing backstage to this scene before me, was as poignant as any memories we created that summer. Only through the humility of this amazing teen and the innocence of children could this powerful and dramatic teaching of God's sovereignty have played out.

God is the potter and we are the clay. Like the pat of butter that is presented for our bread, we can choose to be just a simple pat, or we can be transformed into one of His masterpieces; they are many, each one unique. Someone takes the time to shape our butter. There is an unexpected grace in that. We are all the work of God's hand, made in His likeness, but each one still unique. There is an unexpected grace in that as well.

Lord, thank You for the innocence of children and their openness to both give and receive Your truth with such wonder and grace. Thank You for reminding us of Your sovereignty through precious moments like these; that You are the potter and we are the clay. Young or old, we are all works in progress, still being shaped and transformed into Your likeness. In Jesus' name, amen.

WEEKLY WISDOM WALK

The Bible is full of references to the potter and the clay (Job 10:9, 33:6; Ps. 2:9; Isa. 29:16, 45:9, 64:8; Jer. 18:1; Rom. 9:20–21; Rev. 2:27). Spend time this week reading about God's sovereignty over our lives. That we are here at all is not arbitrary. It is by His grace. Each of us is fearfully and wonderfully made (Ps.

139:14). God has shaped us and continues to shape us until we are transformed into His likeness (2 Cor. 3:18). Ask God to lead you through His Word to those scriptures that will make this real for you. Mark them and hide these words into your heart (Ps. 119:11).

We are God's masterpiece (Eph. 2:10, NLT).

COTTON-CANDY CLOUDS

God's Love

We are God's masterpiece.
—Ephesians 2:10, nlt

Have you ever found yourself waxing nostalgic about favorite childhood memories? No matter what kind of childhood we've had, I bet we can all picture ourselves falling back on a bed of soft green grass for an afternoon of "cloud busting." Remember trying to figure out what shapes the clouds resembled? Maybe you now find yourself resurrecting this game with your children or grandchildren.

Every once in a while, I will see an amazing cloud formation and it will catapult me back to those carefree moments, when I was completely enveloped by God's creation, from the cool grass beneath me to the clouds overhead. Those summer days with the enormous cumulus clouds always made for the best cloud busting. But, the secret to a great game of cloud busting is neither the day nor the clouds. It is the wind! The wind has to be perfect—too much, and the images are fleeting—too little, and the game gets boring. There needs to be just enough wind to keep a steady flow of rabbits, turtles, hearts, and flowers parading across this expanse of blue canvas called sky.

Though particularly enjoyable to play in our youth among friends, there is a renewed joy in sharing this childhood pleasure with your child. My husband, son, and I were driving home one evening when I looked up to the evening sky. It was getting close to dusk. I love this time of night. Often when I am asked, "What is your favorite color?" this is my response, "The color the sky turns just before sunset, a mixture of those incredible hues of pinks and purples, oranges and yellows." On this evening, I found such a manifestation of swirled colors, like a gallon of paint not fully stirred. In the center of the palette was one brushstroke, as if God turned his paintbrush on end and cut a rift in the vibrant tones beginning to blend. Peeking through the slit in the sky was a slice of the setting sun, illuminating the surrounding shades into indescribable saturations. I was willing my husband to drive faster, so I could run to the top of our deck, camera in hand, and attempt to snap a few pictures before the wind stirred the band of colors and the sun set, leaving us again to the dark of night.

In moments, we were home. I motioned to my son, "Grab your camera and follow me!" Together, we scaled the hill behind our home to the deck that looks out over our city, but to my surprise, the twists and turns we took making our way home obscured any view we had of the setting sun peeking through the colorful slice of the heavens. However, what we did discover was the most majestic, incredibly sculpted cotton candy clouds we had ever seen. This was cloud busting at its absolute best! It was as if the circus came to town in the form of clouds and the feature attraction was cotton candy. Big cumulus clouds of pinks, purples, oranges and yellows—all mixed together. We stood there in awe. "Whoa!" my son whispered. This was much better than what we had anticipated. So like God. He gives us much more than we expect or desire out of His great love for us.

The wind was moving along at a pretty good pace. I knew my son and I had to take our pictures quickly. What fun we had! "Look at THAT one." "Check THIS one out!" I looked down at my neighborhood, to those who were playing in their yards or gathering with friends. The thought occurred to me, "I wonder if anyone else is seeing these clouds right now, because in less than a moment, they will be different, busted!" It was then, I felt as if God had created those clouds just for my son and I to share. Isn't it great to know that God loves us that much? To know we are so special to God that He can use His creation to show us how much we mean to Him? Each cloud is a masterpiece, created by God. And, on that night, it was as if He formed one of them for my son and I, to tell us what Paul wrote to the Ephesians. "We are God's masterpiece" as well. Here is a gift. I made this for you, because I love you. A masterpiece for a masterpiece, with love, from your Master.

Master God, I love you. Thank you for loving me unconditionally and for not only providing for my every need, but also for the amazing surprises along our journey together. When I least expect it, You are there with your expressions of great love and reminders of Your presence. Thank You for Your creation and for unhindered, uncontrived moments when I can share it with my child. In Jesus' name I pray, amen.

Weekly Wisdom Walk

Read Ephesians, Chapter 2. Then, try some nostalgia this week. Do something that really brought you great joy. Was it finding a surprise in the bottom of a Cracker Jack box? Dunking Oreos? Making whistles out of a blade of grass? Blowing dandelions? Share this joy with a child—your own child, a relative, or a friend. Or, visit a shelter and spread the joy with some children in need. Give a gift from the Master!

Though she may forget, I will not forget you! See, I have engraved you on the palms of my hands (Isa. 49:15–16).

BLUEBIRDS

Unforsaken Love

Can a mother forget the baby at her breast and have no compassion on the child she has borne? Though she may forget, I will not forget you! See, I have engraved you on the palms of my hands; your walls are ever before me.
—Isaiah 49:15–16

ARE YOU A bird watcher? I have never been a huge fan of birds until I had a child. My son was the first to admire these amazing creatures, a love passed on to him by the former headmaster of his school. Soon, he began collecting the paraphernalia—birdcalls, Audubon Society books, birdsong gadgets. It wasn't long before my husband, the quintessential outdoorsman, acquired a passion for birding as well. Now, we are invested in birdhouses, feeders, and baths and, of course, a banquet of food.

A favorite is the Eastern Bluebird. We watch from the dinner table as the mother and father gather fine twigs, pine needles and various materials to create their nest inside the bluebird house. Afterwards, it is still very much a guessing game for us. Sometimes, the parents abandon the nest, but most of the time we are fortunate enough to see the entire cycle. The father will become more of a central figure in our voyeurism, and we realize the mother is incubating the eggs. Soon, we will see a feverish frenzy of eating. Back and forth they go, feeding their young. Ultimately, silence is restored. To date, we have never seen the baby birds emerge.

During this fledgling stage, the parents will take the birds to a nearby tree in our yard. There, they feed them, teach them how to find food sources and fend for themselves. This is the most treacherous time for a fledgling bluebird, as they are vulnerable to predators. After five weeks, they are on their own as far as food is concerned. However, most, but not all, will continue to stay close to their parents and will travel with them, their extended and future families, in flocks.

After the bluebirds leave their nest, we clean out the birdhouse, awaiting the arrival of the next new family. Sometimes, we wonder if it is the same mother and father who have returned. Where are the juvenile birds while their parents are birthing a new brood? Have they forgotten them temporarily? How many of the fledgling birds survived the five weeks of feeding training?

As a parent, there is no greater love, than the love for a child. It is of this kind of love of which Isaiah speaks, because its meaning is universal. Yet, God loves us more! *"Can a mother forget the baby at her breast and have no compassion on the child she has borne? Though she may forget, I will not forget you! See, I have engraved you on the palms of my hands; your walls are ever before me"* Isaiah 49:15–16.

How many times have you heard this message in someone's testimony? They were lost, and then they were found. They suffered a terrible childhood, a tragedy, wandered away, questioned God, blamed God, even; maybe experienced sickness, abandonment, addiction, injustice. Where was God? The hand of God could not possibly be found in their circumstances. Yet, it is in the looking back that they see it. He was there all along. He never left. He never leaves us, even when we have fledged. He is faithful, when we are unfaithful. God is not like the Eastern Bluebird. He is a forever parent. And though he teaches and may seem distant at times, he will never abandon you. Your walls are ever before Him. It is as the prophet foretold. He has engraved you on the palms of His hands. Now, that's love!

> *Heavenly Father, How can we wrap our minds around such love as this? Though we may be parents as well, we only see through a glass dimly of the kind of love You have for us. It is hard to fathom, but we are humbled and grateful for it. Thank You for Your unwavering, unconditional love. Thank You that we do not have to earn it, it is freely given, and Your only Son paid the price, having the nail-scarred palms to show for it. Help us to be ever mindful of this great love and always appreciative of the gift. In Jesus' name we pray, amen.*

Weekly Wisdom Walk

Have you ever written your testimony? Chronicled the hand of God in your life? How did you come to know Jesus as your Savior? Though you may have told bits and pieces of your story, there is nothing quite like retaking the journey with our Lord and writing it down. If you want to fall in love with the risen Christ all over again, try writing down your walk to Him this week. It may be a linear story or very circuitous with stops and bumps along the way. Whatever it is, it is your journey. God wooed you and pursued you, never giving up on you. It is something to be celebrated. Spend some time loving God back in a different way this week. Relive your walk together and write it down. You will *love* the experience and be blessed by the journey.

In all your ways acknowledge him and he will make your paths straight (Prov. 3:6).

PATH OF THE STORM

Times of Trouble

Trust in the LORD with all your heart and lean not on
your own understanding; in all your ways acknowledge him, and he will make your paths straight.
—PROVERBS 3:5–6

IT WAS AUGUST of 1992, hurricane season. My husband and I were living on Miami Beach at the time. Hurricane Andrew was headed toward us, but no one seemed too alarmed, at first. All hurricanes, spinning recklessly off the coast of Africa, topple towards South Florida. Nevertheless, as this one got closer, it appeared, after many years, this ominous presence was going to make landfall rather than shimmy up the coast like a top.

The beach residents, we among them, were the first to be evacuated. Then, the evacuees were evacuated. Ultimately, we found shelter with friends south of Miami, since the brunt of the storm was to wreak the worst havoc north of us. Novices, not "storm trackers," we weren't experienced in the art of discerning the hurricane's path. It looks something like a child's top or gyro spinning across a hardwood floor. The slightest little ridge and it changes direction. There is nothing straight about it. It is unpredictable. Still, like the millions of Floridians glued to their televisions that day, we heard "go south," so we did.

As these stories tend to go, Hurricane Andrew changed course at the last minute and, you guessed it, headed south. We were directly in the path of the storm, which, that year, became the most destructive hurricane in U.S. history. For seven hours, we ran from room to room as the windows blew out and the storm was, literally, in the home with us. Walls came down, a portion of the roof flew off. Soon we had all scattered, looking for places to hide. My husband and I ended up in a bi-fold linen closet next to the only concrete block wall in the house, thinking it was the one wall that may survive the storm. We leaned hard into that wall, and once we were able to catch our breaths, we spoke to each other and decided we should pray. Overcome by fear, though, the Lord's Prayer became a muddled version of the "Our Father" and the "Pledge of Allegiance!" Our circumstances may have been out of our control, but God was very much in control. Even when we are afraid, He still holds us in the palms of His hands. We trusted in that and held on tight. Eventually, the storm ended and we made it out alive. Many did not.

Is it because they did not have enough faith? Of course not! We don't know why bad things happen. Why natural disasters take the lives of some and not others. Why some are robbed of their lives before we are ready for them to go. We try to understand the incomprehensible and cannot. Often, we blame God.

This is not only true of these destructive storms, but also the everyday storms of life—from the inconvenient tailspins that interrupt the flow of our lives to the storms of greater proportion which tend to devastate our daily existence, the seasons of suffering. This morning, I witnessed a car accident. For one driver, it appeared to be a minor inconvenience. For the other, pacing back and forth, inconsolable, it might possibly have been one more in a long list of grievances during a season of suffering. I don't know. Only God knows. "Every day of my life was recorded in your book. Every moment was laid out before a single day had passed" (Ps. 139:16, NLT). So, I prayed.

It is most important, especially when we are in these paths of life's storms, to "Trust in the LORD with all your heart and lean not on your own understanding; in all your ways acknowledge him, and he will make your paths straight" (Prov. 3:5–6). Unlike the hurricane with its wobble and bobble unpredictability, we have a straight path back to wholeness. The hurricane will always fall apart. It cannot be sustained. But, we can. We may not understand what is happening or why, but if we lean hard into our Savior, He will lead us out. He is stronger than the concrete block wall and His love is mightier than a hurricane.

Gracious God, we praise You for Your sovereignty over our lives. Help us to be mindful that You reign victoriously. Keep our trust firm in You, especially when times are difficult and we begin to doubt. Help us to lean hard into You, not only in the valleys but always. Thank You for Your unwavering love. Help us love others with that much power. In Jesus' name, amen.

Weekly Wisdom Walk

Are you going through a difficult time or facing a difficult decision? Are you finding it challenging to step out in faith? In Proverbs 3, Solomon speaks about the benefits of wisdom. God wants us to use our own ability to reason as well as our gifts in our decision-making, but still, we must acknowledge Him, even if we believe we understand. Sometimes, our own understanding is faulty. If we acknowledge, trust, and lean hard into Him, He will make our paths straight. He will give us the discernment we need. Make a list of everything you have on your plate right now. If there is anything you have not brought to the foot of the cross, spend time doing so this week.

I will rain down bread from heaven for you (Exod. 16:4).

MANNA FROM HEAVEN

Divine Providence

Then the Lord said to Moses, "I will rain down bread from heaven for you.
The people are to go out each day and gather enough for that day. In this
way I will test them and see whether they will follow my instructions."
—EXODUS 16:4

ONE SUMMER VACATION, we were sitting on the deck at our favorite
Florida restaurant. It was low tide and we were fortunate enough to
get a seat right next to the beach. Waiting for our meals to be delivered, we took great pleasure watching the conspicuous ghost crabs burrow into
the sand. As the tides ebbed and flowed, we watched them. Between each wave,
one in particular would come out and forage for food to bring back into his
hole. Only our bread had arrived. Ideal crab fare, we thought.

Instantly, we began to toss a few small morsels over the railing to see what
the crab would do. Oh, how we delighted in this little crab once it first reappeared, presumably at the scent of fresh-baked bread—manna "seemingly"
from heaven! At first, we only threw one piece down at a time, each morsel in
a different direction and slightly farther out. Would the crab find it? Would it
attempt a change in direction? Would it risk getting closer to the surf before
scurrying sideways back to the safety of its home?

The crab passed each test. So, we decided to toss out two morsels. A quandary! Would the crab only grab what it needed or take it all? Did it require
more than we provided? At once, a new crab appeared. Competition! We began
to cheer for each to get a piece of bread. They did, but not always. As our game
continued, sometimes the first crab got more. And, the second left empty
handed.

And, so it was when God tested the Israelites in the desert. He rained down bread from heaven in response to their grumbling and complaining. In the evening, there were quail covering the camp, and in the morning the dew turned to thin flakes of frost, which became the bread they were to gather. Like the crabs, the Israelites didn't recognize this foreign substance at first, but once they did, "some gathered much, some little"... "he who gathered much did not have too much, and he who gathered little did not have too little. Each one gathered as much as he needed" (Exod. 16:17–18).

Now, we understand the crabs would have survived without our bread. In fact, our hope is that our manmade feast did not cause them any physical discomfort. However, there is a lesson in all of this. God provides what we need, whether it is for a day or for eternity. Jesus said, "I am the bread of life" (John 6:48). "I am the living bread that came down from heaven. If anyone eats of this bread, he will live forever. This bread is my flesh, which I will give for the life of the world" (John 6:51).

The Israelites were supposed to go out each day and gather their share of bread for only one day, double on the sixth day to last them through the Sabbath. This bread was temporary. If they hoarded it, the bread would go bad the next morning, with the exception of the bread collected on the sixth day. Many times, people will make kind gestures toward me, often without even knowing it, and it will relieve me of a burden, maybe not of hunger but of busyness or of a heavy heart. Sometimes, I'll express my gratitude with a cheerful, "It's like Manna from Heaven!" It is an incredibly providential gift, but it is also temporary. No less appreciated, but, like the bread, sustaining enough to get me to the next day. We need this kind of grace in our lives, and I'm thankful for those who give it.

Yet, Jesus provides the living bread! "I am the bread of life. He who comes to me will never go hungry, and he who believes in me will never be thirsty (John 6:35).

We are going back to the beach again and will, no doubt, look for the crabs at our favorite restaurant. He created them too. This time, when the bread arrives, I will think of Jesus, the living bread.

Precious Jesus, You are the source of eternal life. Let us never forget what You did for us so that we may live for all eternity with You in Heaven. Each time we break bread, let us remember Your sacrifice and be grateful that we have life in You, and let us glorify You by living it abundantly for You. In Your name we pray, amen.

Weekly Wisdom Walk

Pray for God to reveal himself to you in scripture this week. Read Exodus, Chapter 16, and then John, Chapter 6. Compare and contrast the two readings. What does this teach you about God's Divine providence and about obedience? Journal any other truths the Lord places on your heart this week.

Don't obey them only to please them when they are watching. Be sure your heart does what God wants (Eph. 6:6, NIV).

STARFISH

Evangelism

Don't obey them only to please them when they are watching. Do it
because you are slaves of Christ. Be sure your heart does what God wants.
—EPHESIANS 6:6

HAVE YOU EVER read the "Starfish Story?" It is a delightful little story,
watered down over the years from a piece written by author, Loren
Eiseley. However, the Internet version is about a young man, sometimes a woman or girl, who is found saving starfish washed ashore. It is the
"one at a time" notion of salvation to which the reader is drawn. It's a timeless
story. One which can be read again and again, at various junctures in your life's
journey, each time leaving you answering another question or, perhaps, asking
a new one.

My husband experienced as much while on vacation this summer. A hurricane churned up the Atlantic, never making landfall, but creating enough of
a disturbance to alter the marine life and beach treasures during our annual
visit. He was the first to awake and voyage over the dunes down to the ocean.
As he strolled along the uninhabited shoreline allowing the tides to welcome
him with an enticing ebb and flow, he saw them. Bright blue starfish—every
few strides—were caressing the coastline. Starfish that might have baked in the
hot, Florida sunshine while waiting for the next high tide, were it not for my
husband reaching down and casting them back, one by one, out to sea.

Like the man in the story, God has cultivated a humble and gentle spirit
within my husband. Like Paul's point to the Ephesians, he seeks not to please
others who are watching. In fact, no one was watching, as he tossed these beautiful creatures back home.

As the days sauntered past, we found ourselves, at one time or another, in different philosophical discussions. One day, he was struggling. He was thinking about an upcoming mission trip and pondering the tenets of the Great Commission—in particular, evangelism. "Do I do enough to bring others to Christ?" he wondered. Again, I think of him, the Starfish, and this "one at a time" notion of salvation. I also thought of Andrew, the first disciple.

While Peter preached to thousands, "making disciples of all nations" (Matt. 28:19), it was Andrew who brought Peter, one man, to Christ. Peter added three thousand to the church at Pentecost (Acts 2:41), but had it not been for Andrew, Peter may not have known Jesus. Andrew, although a background disciple, was a "one at a time" kind of guy. He did what was right, when no one was watching. He was the quintessential servant. He was always sure his heart did what God wanted. He brought Peter to Jesus (John 1:40–42), and he also brought the boy with the five loaves and two fish to Jesus (John 6:8–9). It was Andrew who brought that which Jesus would use to feed the five thousand.

It only takes one disciple, who believes Jesus is who He says He is. It only takes one "Andrew" willing to approach one potential follower, because we don't know if that follower is going to be the next Peter. It only takes one with a heart sure of what God wants and a laser focus on His sovereignty. It is as Oswald Chambers so beautifully crafted in *My Utmost for His Highest*, "One life totally devoted to God is of more value to Him than one hundred lives which have been simply awakened by His Spirit."

My husband is an "Andrew." There are many more starfish in the sea this week because of him, but no one would know it had I not written this. Souls will be won for Christ, maybe directly, maybe in a ripple effect, because of God's work through my husband's humble service. But, no one will know about that, either, no one except the One who made him into His likeness. That's because; my husband "Doesn't obey.. only to please them when they are watching," but "because [he] is a slave of Christ...sure [his] heart does what God wants" (Eph. 6:6).

> *Precious heavenly Father, thank You for the blessing of marriage and godly men to do life with. What a treasure You have given us! Help us to be mindful of this gift and not to hinder our spouse's walk with You in any way. Show us how to encourage our husbands and be the wives You intended us to be. Continue to grow in our husbands—humility, gentleness, and faith. In Your Son, Jesus' name, amen*

WEEKLY WISDOM WALK

There are only nine references to Andrew in the Bible. Read about him this week. Notice when the Greeks approach Philip to see Jesus, Philip takes them to Andrew. It is Andrew who takes them to Jesus. For as little as we know about Andrew, we can glean from Scripture that Andrew has a relationship with Jesus that is special. It exemplifies the kind of relationship, I think, Jesus wants all of us to have—one of authenticity and complete accessibility. Spend some time this week relationally with Jesus, whatever form that means for you. Experience the oneness and the wholeness that comes from communing with our Lord and Savior. Begin to discover who you uniquely are in Christ.

THE STARFISH STORY

Original Story by: Loren Eiseley

One day a man was walking along the beach when he noticed
a boy picking something up and gently throwing it into the ocean.
Approaching the boy, he asked, "What are you doing?"
The youth replied, "Throwing starfish back into the ocean.
The surf is up and the tide is going out. If I don't throw them back,
     they'll die."
"Son," the man said, "don't you realize there are miles and miles of
     beach and hundreds of starfish? You can't make a difference!"
After listening politely, the boy bent down, picked up another starfish,
and threw it back into the surf. Then, smiling at the man, he said..."
I made a difference for that one."

And if anyone gives even a cup of cold water to one of these little ones … he will certainly not lose his reward (Matt. 10:42).

THIRSTY, LITTLE TREE

Giving and Receiving

And if anyone gives even a cup of cold water to one of
these little ones because he is my disciple, I tell you the
truth, he will certainly not lose his reward.
—MATTHEW 10:42

IN THE SOUTHEAST, we recently recovered from a drought. It seems, every few years, we go through a cycle of drought seasons—two, three, or four years in a row, sometimes. The trees get very thirsty. Usually when this happens, we are on a complete watering ban. Often we can water by hand or on a schedule, but such allowances do nothing for the trees. They need big water, rainwater.

This latest drought began the first summer after we renovated the backyard landscape at our new home. Of course, the one thing needed to care for our transplanted bushes, trees, and new additions is the one thing we lack, rain. Still, we have enjoyed the transformation of the once dirt and green, now vibrant with colorful splendor. We started to see the distress. One thirsty, little tree in particular did not appear to be winning the battle being waged. The tiniest of the Crepe Myrtles framing our yard, she was transplanted into a shadier spot and required a bit more sun like the others are afforded. Her leaves began turning fall colors in mid summer, and she did not produce her beautiful pink blossoms as the others had.

Yet, nature has a way of taking care of such things. Not always, but most often for me, when I am purposefully present and taking notice of them. By late summer, hurricane season was upon us, and while we are not directly in the path any longer, we do get the outer bands of the winds and rains on occasion.

For a week, the rain finally came, bringing the drink of water so desperately needed to the parched land of our region. It was when the sky emptied its last cup of cold water; I noticed our thirsty, little tree was no longer thirsty. Branches outstretched to heaven above, adorned in pink blooms—a reward, an offering, a gift of a grateful heart worn on the outside for all to see.

I thought of the encouragement offered in Matthew, "And if anyone gives even a cup of cold water to one of these little ones because he is my disciple, I tell you the truth, he will certainly not lose his reward" (Matt. 10:42). A friend of mine is battling cancer. Many of us, wearing our pink ribbons and "strive for a cure" wristbands, are reaching out to her with a cup of cold water. She is the "little one," not because she is small in stature, child-like, frail, or fragile. That is not what Jesus meant. She is the "little one" because she is a disciple of Christ. By seeing her through this time, in an expression of solidarity, we too, are received by Christ and will not lose our reward.

I am not what you would call a "girly-girl." I am not a "pink" person. But, lately, because of my sweet friend and her journey, I am surrounded, gratefully, by pink. And, this week, the reminder of my reward in heaven came dressed up in the most heavenly pink flowers from a once thirsty, little tree, which thirsts no more. Because of all who are receiving the call to bring a cup of cold water, my precious friend will thirst no more. Her branches will not show distress. The light will not be unable to reach her. It will be brought to her. Still, it can barely supplement the light that emanates from her. She is a strong little one, like my tree, and one day soon, she will be reaching, once again, with her arms outstretched to the heavens above, adorned in pink, with an offering, a gift—her grateful heart worn on the outside for all to see.

Gracious and Merciful God, You are our Healer, from withering trees on sun-baked lands to suffering "little ones" with hearts set firmly on You. God, I am so moved by Your majesty and Your sovereignty over all things. Wherever I go, You are there. I am incredibly humbled and grateful for Your perfect reminders of how present You are in every situation. Thank You for Your divine whispers to our hearts and for the visual reminders that You are here in the middle of our circumstances. Help us all to live each day by the example of Your Son, Jesus—for the cups of cold water given and received. In His name we pray, amen.

Weekly Wisdom Walk

Read Matthew 10:40–42. This is part of Jesus' speech to the disciples as He sends them out to do His works. This portion of the scripture talks about giving and receiving, not making grand gestures but starting with a "cup of cold water" for example. Jesus did not commission them to start by going off to far-away lands, but instead begin in their own backyards, so to speak, with the lost and confused. Is there anyone in your life, right now, who might need a "cup of cold water?" Someone once told me, don't ask, "Is there anything I can do?" Instead, just think of something you can do, and do it! Pray about it. Start small. You might be surprised where this takes you.

Do not forget to entertain strangers, for by so doing some people have entertained angels without knowing it (Heb. 13:2).

MARJORIE'S SMILE

Hospitality

Do not forget to entertain strangers, for by so doing some
people have entertained angels without knowing it.
—HEBREWS 13:2

I HAVE ALWAYS DREAMED of going to Africa. Is there any idealistic American
with thoughts of saving the world who has not? I have had opportunities
to be involved in service-related projects that benefit Africa, but I'm still
waiting to travel there. At some point, I think I tucked away my dream and
moved on to smaller ones, until one night, almost two years ago.

I had decided to attend a ladies gathering at church. The goal was to create
small groups that would meet regularly throughout the next year or two, in
lieu of Sunday school—community groups with whom we could study curric-
ulum and grow relationally with each other and with our Lord Jesus. New to
the church, I had a visual in mind of what my new group of friends would
be like. I decided it would be a coffee klatch of my peers—same season of
life, same area of town, same life issues, middle-aged with children, fighting
off menopause, too young for senior discounts, too old for Abercrombie and
Fitch, and maybe, within spitting distance of each other on our spiritual
walk. God had other plans.

Most of the women attending needed an evening group. Only a handful of
the hundred or so participants needed a morning group. I was among them.
The playing field got very narrow, very quickly. Of those remaining, half could
meet on Tuesday, half on Thursday. My Tuesday group was formed in the blink
of an eye. As I looked around, though, this was not the group in my mind's
eye. Not only did we represent every season of life, more than three decades

between us, but we drew from every corner of Atlanta. Our spiritual walks were circuitous, from infancy to more seasoned and back again, with stops and deviations in between. There was one older woman, however, who was not partial to Tuesdays or Thursdays and just stood at the intersection of the two morning groups, looking very regal and peaceful in her African headdress, saying nothing as many of us, all talking at once, tried to hammer out logistics.

I heard an inner voice, a still, small voice, speak to my heart, "Go to her." Whether you turn to the right or to the left, your ears will hear a voice behind you, saying, "This is the way; walk in it" (Isa. 30:21). Her name is Marjorie. I did not know it then, but she had attempted to leave the meeting several times that evening. She had been out for a walk and only came in thinking there was a church service. She looked around the room and felt like a stranger, like she didn't belong. Each time she attempted to leave, someone would encourage her to return.

By the end of the evening, I was in a small group. It was not the coffee klatch I envisioned. We had no leader. We had no idea where we were going to meet. Finding a central location was our first task. Marjorie was visiting from Zambia on a three-year visa and could not drive. We had many hurdles to overcome. This was not what I had planned. God had other plans.

But, hurdles are overcome, with a little ingenuity and a lot of prayer. In record time, this incredibly eclectic group of women, at first complete strangers, became the most authentic, transparent group of disciples for Christ with whom I have ever had the pleasure of learning and growing. Most remarkable was the friendship that developed between Marjorie and me, born from a Divine whisper to "go to her." I became Marjorie's transportation at first, but in those rides filled with infectious conversation, sometimes wrought with emotion, a deep abiding friendship grew from the mere seed I believe God planted.

Marjorie does not work and has no money. She has many needs. In contrast, I have means and can afford to provide certain things for her. But, quite honestly, when it comes to giving, Marjorie has much to offer. Jesus said, "I tell you the truth, whatever you did for one of the least of these brothers of mine, you did for me" (Matt. 25:40). There are times when others presume to know who is "the least" in our relationship—who is the giver and who is the receiver. Materially, yes, I have more. Yet, there was a time, when I was very sick with pneumonia and she called me and prayed over the phone in her native tongue, Bemba, and then sang to me like a mother to a child. Like a woman with only a jar of perfume for Jesus, Marjorie shares with me all that she has. She gives from a trifle. I give out of abundance. Who, though, has given more of themselves?

At the end of our first year together, my small group approached me. They wanted to give Marjorie a gift. Most of Marjorie's teeth were lost in a tragic bus accident in Africa. Many were killed. Her own brother died after taking her to the hospital, so she never had a chance to complete the work. Immediately we got to work on finding a way to repair Marjorie's teeth, and with the help of some friends, we were able to pool our resources and accomplish our goal. It is humbling to see the strength of the human spirit in Marjorie and the humanity of each person who participated in this ministry. At one point, I noticed even the parking attendant next to the train station had stopped charging me to park while I waited for her arrival. Many people became involved, over nine months, in Marjorie's smile.

Personally, I will never forget her toothless one. She beams with the love of Jesus. When I see her approaching my car, it is like a beacon of light and peace. I feel her excitement as her wide-open smile lights up her precious face. Nevertheless, Marjorie prayed for new teeth, and my small group wanted her to have them. All I dreamed of was going to Africa. God had other plans. He brought Africa to me—in a stranger—named Marjorie. "Do not forget to entertain strangers, for by so doing some people have entertained angels without knowing it" (Heb. 13:2).

Gracious God, thank You for Marjorie and thank You for not always answering our prayers in the way we have asked. You are all-knowing and have our best interests at heart. Help me to trust in that truth forever. Lord, I ask for Your blessings on all of the Marjories of the world, all of those who give generously from so little and for the incredible faith they model, that unwavering faith that no matter what the circumstances, no matter how long we have to wait, that You are listening to us, You are here, available, approachable, a whisper in prayer away. Bless those who recognize the weak, the lost, the broken, "the least" and come out of the woodwork to lend a hand or a handful to help. In Jesus' name we pray, amen.

WEEKLY WISDOM WALK

Who are the "angels" in your life? Spend some time this week identifying and acknowledging them in some way. Often it is in looking back that we see how God placed someone in our path to teach us about Himself, His Word, about us or His plan for us. In Hebrews 13:2, the author is speaking, specifically, about hospitality. Entertaining strangers was crucial in biblical culture. Inns were expensive, so believers opened their doors to travelers spreading the gospel. We have opportunities, today, to house those visiting from other countries, on mission trips and in youth groups. However, we can also show our hospitality towards someone through our disposition and the way we receive them. Practice Christ-like hospitality this week, particularly in the company of strangers. You just might find yourself entertaining an angel.

Summer/Fall

...and the heavens will drop their dew (Zech. 8 :12).

MAKING A DIFFERENCE

Service, Obedience

The seed will grow well, the vine will yield its fruit, the ground will
produce its crops, and the heavens will drop their dew. I will give
all these things as an inheritance to the remnant of this people.
—Zechariah 8:12

L AST YEAR, I revisited Bosnia on a mission trip. I returned overwhelmed
by this once thriving culture, still in its post war-torn state, more than
a decade since civil unrest brought a country and a people to its knees.
We traveled as a team with great hopes to bring encouragement to our partner
Christians, so desperately trying to make a difference in the midst of this
brokenness. To a pastor and church, who see a country on its knees, join them
on bended knee, not in hopelessness but in the unwavering hopefulness we
have in a Savior who has promised to restore His people, save them, and bestow
abundant blessings upon them. Still, I was distracted. My eyes were drawn to
the remnants of war; the bombed-out shells of buildings, which once repre-
sented thriving business and a bustling economy. I ached as I gazed upon the
schoolhouses riddled with bullet holes beneath classroom windows, as I heard
the sounds of screaming children in my head. I wanted so desperately to be an
encourager as I prayed alongside our new friends in Christ, but wondered how
effective I could be as I mourned the wounds of a nation and a people so deeply
inside. Knowing it was God's call, which brought me to this beautiful country
and these amazingly resilient people, I prayed for God to guide me through
the range of emotions and give me the strength, the words to be a support to
them.

I likened my initial visit to Bosnia as making a new friend with a severely scarred face. I assumed, once you fall in love with your new friend, you no longer see the wounds, but the heart. You will see as God sees. It is true. Returning for my second visit, I began to reminisce over my photos and found not a single pockmark in a single frame. My photo journal captured the hearts of the people, our laughs, and our cries together. I dove deeper into relationship with them, giddy as a schoolgirl to be reunited, as I watched each one approach and broken to tears to bid farewell upon leaving. With each visit, I believe I leave a bit of my heart behind. In fact, I do not know who is providing the encouragement really. These are a people, so simple in their faith, so appreciative for life, so grateful to have a job, to have woken up this morning. They delight in their children instead of scold them. They pray for a hedge of protection around them every day, as opposed to only desiring it, as the need is real. Their faith is without question stronger than my own. They praise before supplication and punctuate their need with love and thankfulness for a faithful and sovereign God who is true to His promises, even the ones He has yet to supply, but they are certain He will. I do not know that I offer anything, teach much, provide any service or fulfill a need, but they do seem grateful for our presence. I can only hope it is because they see our Lord Jesus in us. I hope to return soon. I cannot honestly say if I am returning for myself or for them—for me or for God. I only know I must go back. I am called to this country and to these people.

As I glanced through my photos, there was one that captured my eye. There is always one. A picture I took for no apparent reason other than it seemed powerful in the moment. I did not know why, but I knew I soon would. The image was of a dewdrop clinging above the lush fertile green ground. How I loved to watch dewdrops as a child. I would watch them until they would get heavy enough to drop off and be counted. They would matter at that point; potentially make a difference, providing nourishment to what lay beneath. Maybe it's not much, but a start. One drop. Much like our presence in Bosnia. Who is being nourished? I do not know. Perhaps, I am just a drop of dew. But, if God could use a drop of dew to restore Israel, maybe there is a chance he could use me as well. "The seed will grow well, the vine will yield its fruit, the ground will produce its crops, and the heavens will drop their dew. I will give all these things as an inheritance to the remnant of this people" (Zech. 8:12).

Heavenly Father, how mighty You are that You could use drops of dew from the heavens to bring about restoration. Let us be forever grateful for the renewal and replenishment we find in You and the inheritance we are promised in Your kingdom. Help us to give You glory by bringing Your kingdom here on Earth every day through our words, thoughts and actions, and most of all, through our love, lived out boldly. In Jesus' name, amen.

WEEKLY WISDOM WALK

As a child, did you ever watch water drip from the end of a garden hose, watching and counting each drop until it completely stopped? Do you ever feel that small, as if your impact matters little? Consider a drip from a faucet into a water-clogged sink. Have you ever noticed the ripple effect? Even the tiniest movement can make a widespread difference for Christ. This week create a ripple effect. Offer a smile, a prayer, send a card. Think about how a tiny gesture might have a far-reaching effect.

For this reason I remind you to fan into flame the gift of God, which is in you through the laying on of my hands (2 Tim. 1:6).

RESERVOIR OR CANAL?

Gifts

For this reason I remind you to fan into flame the gift of God,
which is in you through the laying on of my hands.
—2 TIMOTHY 1:6

I
T IS THE anniversary week that marks a date of questionable celebra-
tion. This week my mentor and best friend has spent as many years out of
ordained ministry as he spent in it. That is it. That is all I received in my
e-mail. A simple sentence, yet there is so much more lying beneath the surface
of those typed words.

This is a man who led me to Christ and has been my adviser for nearly two
decades. He has touched as many lives out of the pulpit as he did in it. The
same week my dear friend has been pondering the synergy of a ministry, I have
been grappling with a spiritual thought nugget that keeps resurfacing in my
studies—is it better to be a reservoir or a canal? There are many pithy quotes on
the subject. If you want to be wise, be a reservoir and wait until you are filled.
Nourish out of abundance. Still another suggests a canal to be best. In this way,
we are simply aligning ourselves with God and becoming empty vessels. There
is no need to concern ourselves with supply issues. God provides.

If we store up, before we minister to those in need, are we wasting time?
Will we only reap what we sow and not sow as much, or will we accomplish
more? In contrast, if we are canals, with nothing reserved from which to draw,
will we continue to be replenished with an inexhaustible supply, making the
reservoir obsolete? What a challenge! I have been amazed at how many times
this theme has come up in my reading. Even more surprising is how many
authors have biblical backup for their theories. Frankly, I don't know who is

"right?" I'm thinking this is pretty subjective. God probably does what He does and we can't place a formula to it. I'm quite sure if I chose to be a reservoir, He'd decide I would have made a better canal, or vice versa. So, on this one, I'm going to just continue to place it on my list of questions to bring to Heaven!

Nevertheless, as I celebrated my own anniversary, a birthday, I looked down at my birthday candles and found the answer, which my special friend might have offered. While I had been struggling back and forth with the answers: "reservoir? No, canal? No." I heard His voice in my head... "It is neither a reservoir nor a canal. It is a flame." I laughed! So like him, of course! He would have some completely different spin on how to dispense our God-given gifts and blessings, be it tangible or intangible. Almost immediately, I recalled a scripture he used in a blessing he led for our two families at the beach one summer: "fan into flame the gift of God, which is in you...". We don't have to "become" anything. We already have the flame in us! As he described one summer, there are certain things we have that can be taken from us. Water is an example of such a thing. If we have a glass of water—or a reservoir for that matter—and we gave some away, we would have less. But, as followers of Christ Jesus, we have an inextinguishable fire inside of us. Like a candle, we can give away some of our fire and still possess the same amount. A reservoir can dry up. A canal only disburses what it receives, but the fire of Christ Jesus burning in us—this gift, if fanned into flame will continue to burn, and we can give it away all we want without depleting the source. Maybe I won't need to put this one on my list after all!

Ministry is not confined to the pulpit anymore than church is confined to a building. It is about God's people fanning the flame of the gifts they have been given, and then going out and, with that flame, winning those souls for Jesus. I am grateful for my sweet friend who continues to exemplify this with his life.

Abba Father, You are so incredible and awesome. Thank You for giving us the freedom to worship You and ask all of the heady questions, even if we never figure out the answers to them. Thank You for listening to us and for allowing us to have a relationship with You and for giving us amazing people that we can share life with, journeying through both mountaintops and valleys. We praise You and pray all of this in your precious son Jesus' name, amen

WEEKLY WISDOM WALK

Before there were pulpits and church buildings on every street corner, there were simple ordinary men, followers of Christ, going out into the world and fanning the flame that was in them—"death defeated, life vindicated in a steady blaze of light, all through the work of Jesus" (2 Tim. 1:10, THE MESSAGE). "Guard this precious thing placed in your custody by the Holy Spirit who works in us" (2 Tim. 1:14, THE MESSAGE). Also, read Paul's letter to Timothy, "Encouragement to be Faithful" (2 Tim. 1:3–2:13). What can you do to fan the flame this week? Do you have a mentor who brought you to Christ or has helped you grow spiritually? Think of ways you might honor him or her over the next few days.

Waiting does not diminish us (Rom. 8:23–25, THE MESSAGE).

SNAIL'S PACE

Patience

...waiting does not diminish us; any more than waiting diminishes a pregnant mother. We are enlarged in the waiting. We,
of course, don't see what is enlarging us. But the longer we wait,
the larger we become, and the more joyful our expectancy.
—ROMANS 8:23–25, THE MESSAGE

I AM NOT A patient person. My husband says I have two speeds—0 and 99 mph. I walk fast and I talk fast. When I was first starting out, working in corporate America, I would buzz around the office and people would, literally, move to the side as I came through. My co-workers used to tease me, saying the reason I wore contacts is because they have not invented glasses that could handle my G-forces. Of course, this was decades ago. Upon becoming a Christian as well as looking the age of fifty in the face, I have learned to appreciate the art of slowing.

Still, on occasion, I find myself falling into the "hurry" trap from time to time. Most often I am impatient with things, rather than people. In the New Testament, the Greek translation used two different words for patience—patience with circumstances and patience with people. I find people easier. We can always say, politely, "Geez, Mrs. Talksalot, I am really enjoying this conversation, but I need to get to school and pick up my child, do you mind if we finish this at another time?" On a good day, I hope my words will be as pleasant and worthy. Patience with circumstances is completely different to me. We need mercy there. Many times we are simply captive, with no options, but waiting. We require patience, divine patience sometimes.

This morning, I was lost in thought about all the little inconveniences causing me to wait—traffic lights making that turn from amber to ruby red, the school bus with lights blinking just on the verge of flipping the metal arm stop sign, the distant sound of a train whistle together with the first flash of crossings lights and signals sounding, rush-hour and back-to-school traffic. On and on I went through my list. Of course, waiting patiently or not is the choice I have to make. I did rather well today, but only because I was deliberately testing myself. It was a contemplative exercise, a proactive thought put into action, not a reactive response to an annoyance.

Yesterday, I waited too, and today, I wait again... waiting of a different sort. I have been waiting for news. A dear friend of mine is having surgery today. She has been waiting for all sorts of things lately—test results, doctor calls, healing, and, probably, a fair amount of issues of a more spiritual nature—answered prayer, perhaps, a sense of hope on some days, a sense of power on others, and, no doubt, a good measure of patience herself. Thinking of her made me take stock of how trivial my circumstances are in comparison to the big things that many are waiting on, and for, every day.

Waiting is hard. Some days, it is harder than others. The day just seems to drag along at a snail's pace. It seems I have hit every roadblock possible and I wonder if God is intentionally trying to teach me patience on those days. Surprisingly, the little things are the most difficult for me, mostly because either my mind is not focused on the bigger picture, or I have ordered my day incorrectly. But, somewhere, I made a wrong choice. My perspective somehow got turned upside down. I am missing a moment, already thinking of the next one—where I should be, what I am wanting instead of what I already have. A moment longer at a traffic light, or a train track or behind a bus, gives me extra moments with my child, to connect eye to eye in conversation.

Paul wrote to the Romans about enduring our suffering and frustrations in this life and how they cannot compare to the future glory we have in Christ. This is a powerful message coming from someone who suffered great afflic-tion. What strikes me most about his words is the hope, which comes from the waiting. It presents a paradigm shift I had not considered. Like the expectant mother, not always feeling her best for the nine months of pregnancy, it is through the waiting—because of it, not in spite of it, that she ultimately receives her joy. "Waiting does not diminish us; any more than waiting diminishes a pregnant mother. We are enlarged in the waiting. We, of course, don't see what is enlarging us. But the longer we wait, the larger we become, and the more joyful our expectancy" (Rom. 8:23–25).

My sweet friend will endure some suffering and frustration in the months ahead. She will require much healing, much grace, and plenty of mercy. All of this will necessitate her need to draw from a well of patience, only achievable through the Holy Spirit who lives within us. It is accessible to all of us, even to those who lose sight of the big picture while moving at a snail's pace in traffic.

Merciful Father, forgive me. I fall before You, guilty of "hurry sickness" when so many others are waiting for things of far greater importance. Illness, disease, rescue from harm or addiction... waiting for runaway children and parents to return home, for soldiers to return safely from war. Send us your grace, Oh God. We know You weep for Your children. Let us feel Your presence in a way that is manifest and real to us. And, in our waiting, Lord, help our faith to grow richer, larger, deeper, and more resolute. In Jesus' name, we pray, amen.

Weekly Wisdom Walk

Read Romans 8:18–27, "Future Glory." Some consider Romans the jeweled ring of the Bible, and Romans 8, the diamond in the center. You may want to read the entire chapter. Patience is part of the fruit of the Spirit within us. "But the fruit of the Spirit is love, joy, peace, *patience*, kindness, goodness, faithfulness, gentleness and self-control" (Gal. 5:22–23, emphasis added). Notice the word fruit is singular. This is because the Holy Spirit is likened to a bunch of grapes, all of these traits manifest at once, not separately! We can't do that alone. We must call on the One who dwells within us. "Wait on the Lord; Be of good courage, And He shall strengthen your heart; Wait, I say, on the Lord" (Ps. 27:14, NKJV).

...and star differs from star in splendor (1 Cor. 15:41).

THE STAR

Resurrection

The sun has one kind of splendor, the moon another and the
stars another; and star differs from star in splendor.
—1 CORINTHIANS 15:41

HAVE YOU EVER had the privilege of catching a glimpse of some tiny piece of the universe through the eyes of a child? Often these moments can have far-reaching, profound implications. It was such an occasion that brought Paul's lesson about the resurrected body alive for me.

My son and I were taking pictures in our backyard. I was trying to capture a shot by the waterfall and he was going to help. With cameras in hand, we scaled the steps of the steep hill we call a yard and maneuvered our way around the landscape, trying to reach the source of the waterfall. Quickly, I noticed my son was not with me. Something along the way had caught his attention— something much more wonderful to him. In a flashback, I pondered how this had simply become an older version of the toddler more interested in the box and the ribbon than the contents. Try as I might, I couldn't steer him to the waterfall. He was drawn to the summer flowers bursting forth from their buds following a day of sunshine. More intriguing, still, were those, which had run their cycle, become weak and perished—petals fallen to the pine straw below becoming nature's own potpourri.

I watched as my son snapped shot after shot of a barren flower, now only a remnant star of sepals, which once held delicate rose petals. "Look, it's a star," he shouted. Stars fascinate children. Any adult would have passed by this dead flower and scoured the hill for the splendor instead. I still can't get the image out of my head, my son stooped down amidst a sea of colorful blossoms and a vibrant flow of cascading water, mesmerized, by a dead flower. He continued to take picture upon picture, from every angle. "Where, O death, is your victory? Where, O death, is your sting?" (1 Cor. 15:55). For my son, there was no victory or sting in death. This experience was very much alive! It was then that the message of the resurrected life began to percolate. Next year, we will prune this perishable bush and it will rise again, in power and glory. There will be a branch where this same rose once bloomed upon, but it will have a new rose. It will look different in some ways but not all. This is also true of us. Just as the seed must die to produce the plant, we must die to ourselves to be resurrected in Christ Jesus. And, when our physical bodies, wither and die, we will live for all eternity with our Savior, imperishable, raised in power and glory, never again subject to sin or illness. We, too, will be different in some ways, but not in all.

Looking back at my son's photos, I now view the perishing flower in this new light. No longer the physical body it once was, perishable, but a foreshadowing of the resurrected body, depicted by the star, a heavenly, spiritual body. In death, we have life—the resurrected life we will all experience through our Lord Jesus. As seeds, we are planted, die, grow, perish, transform, and are resurrected anew; from Earthly bodies to heavenly ones. "The sun has one kind of splendor, the moon another and the stars another; and star differs from star in splendor" (1 Cor. 15:41).

Lord Jesus, Thank You for taking away the sins of the world and in so doing taking away the sting of death so that we might live in splendor with You. Thank You for making each of us as unique as the stars and for the eyes of a child, a unique lens all of its own. In Your name we pray, amen.

Weekly Wisdom Walk

Do you think we will recognize each other in heaven? Write a list of questions that you have about our heavenly bodies. Then, read Paul's teachings on the Resurrection Body (1 Cor. 15:35–58). Journal your thoughts about our physical bodies vs. our heavenly bodies. Write or speak a prayer to Jesus based on what you have read. Spend the week in grateful praise to our Heavenly Father for taking away the sting of death. Praise Him each time you encounter a dead flower this week.

"You see the people crowding against you," his disciples answered, "and yet you can ask, 'Who touched me?'" (Mark 5:31).

OVERWHELMED

Prayer

At once Jesus realized that power had gone out from him. He
turned around in the crowd and asked, "Who touched my
clothes?" "You see the people crowding against you," his disciples answered, "and yet you can ask, 'Who touched me?'"
—MARK 5:30–31

THEY SAY YOU can tell the age of a tree by the number of rings pressing in around its core. The more encircling it, the more seasoned the tree. This is the image that comes to my mind as I consider the current season of my life. I have reached the time when many of my friends, or their children, are now struck by grave illness. I attend more funerals, deliver more meals, and spend more time in supplication than in praise. My world seems a bit turned unfavorably on axis. I feel overwhelmed by the magnitude of suffering souls. More a stream of consciousness prayer warrior, I am left wondering if I have left someone off of my mental list today as I go to our merciful Father in petition. I count on His knowing the meditations of my heart on most days of late.

I wonder why I make promises I cannot keep. "I will pray for you." Unless I have a pen and paper, I have to rely on memory in those fleeting conversations. Is it just me? Or, do we all fall prey to this spiritual blunder? What is our alternative? "I may not pray for you? I don't have a pen! I might forget." We could run to our cars or homes and jot down another name, I suppose. I'm sure there are many solutions. Still, I don't know if this is the crux of the problem. I am simply overwhelmed. I am overwhelmed by the sheer numbers of those in tragic times and become frozen, unable to pray at all. I lean hard into my

Savior and the Spirit within me who "intercedes for us with groans that words cannot express" (Rom. 8:26).

Crowds surrounded Jesus all the time. Those hoping for healing were continually at His feet. In one story, Jesus was almost crushed by a crowd, when a bleeding woman squeezed through the suffering seekers to touch His cloak. Jesus, at the epicenter of this circle of sickness and sorrow, felt the power leave Him. His power was being depleted! Jesus knew someone had touched Him.

Was Jesus overwhelmed? Maybe. But, significant to me is He felt His power leave Him. When I am frozen in prayer, my list lengthy, I feel powerless. I have come before my Savior, and I have no words. I don't even recall all the names of those for whom I am petitioning anymore. There are too many of them. But, in that very moment I hear another story of cancer, a child's death, or a tragic accident, someone has touched me as well. I know I am called, like Jesus, to have compassion. But, my power is not like His power. My strength is unlike His. Therein lays my problem.

In my arrogance, I have likened myself to Jesus, as if my loved ones have come to me for healing. They have not. A prayer and a pot roast may restore and replenish in part, but not in full. So many of us, as caregivers, try to become the hands and feet of Jesus. It is a valiant and noble gesture. We are called to be like Him, but we are not Him. When we are overwhelmed because our power is depleted, it is an earthly power, not a heavenly one. I am not Jesus in the story. I am the bleeding woman. I must find my power in the hem of His garment, just as she, while my loved ones encircle Him, seeking His healing.

We have conditioned ourselves to believe we must, must, must. We should. We do to our own undoing until there is nothing left for others. We become overwhelmed, then overwrought, and are no benefit to those who need us to be like Jesus to them. We, too, need to be restored and replenished, daily, through the touch of His garment.

Loving Lord, Divine Healer, You call us to care for one another, yet we are so ill equipped. Give us the strength and endurance to comfort and encourage others and Your heart to do it. Teach us how to lead others to Your mighty embrace where real restoration and replenishment resides. Each day, guide us to the hem of Your garment and renew our strength. In Jesus' name, amen.

WEEKLY WISDOM WALK

Are you a caregiver? How do you stay replenished? Do you keep a physical or mental list of those you minister to? Consider your ministry to others. Is it effective? Who are you trying to be in the story? Spend some time with Jesus this week. Ask Him how you can better serve the kingdom through your caring ministry, while keeping yourself spiritually nourished. Make extra effort to touch the hem of His garment every day this week.

However, as it is written: No eye has seen, no ear has heard, no mind has conceived what God has prepared (1 Cor. 2:9).

SEPIA-COLORED GLASSES

God's Eyes

However, as it is written: No eye has seen, no ear has heard, no mind
has conceived what God has prepared for those who love him.
—1 CORINTHIANS 2:9

RECENTLY I BOUGHT a pair of cheap sunglasses. They were the only
semi-fashionable ones on the rack at the gas station and, although I
typically go for the dark black shades, these were sepia in color. Still, I
was desperate. It was an incredibly bright day and the sun was blinding.

The next day, as I was driving my son to school, I noticed the fall color
had really popped. Must have been the freeze we had overnight, I thought.
Each day that week, my drive to and from school was spectacular. I took a
more scenic road one day and just drank in the jaw-dropping beauty of the
hues—deep reds, purples, and particularly the oranges, which seemed overly
plentiful this year.

Days passed before there were any clouds, which required me to lower my
sunglasses in the excessively shady spots of my commute. It was then I realized the fall color was not quite so spectacular after all. It was the perspective
I was given through my sepia-colored glasses. The dead leaves didn't look dead
with the glasses on. They were alive—a vivid orange. The green ones were just
starting to turn. Add sepia to red and the manifestation is even richer.

There was no death in autumn this week for me, only life. Life with grandeur of color, majestic and rich.

As I drove along taking the glasses on and off, back and forth, comparing
and contrasting, I sat in wonderment... "I wonder if this is what God sees?"

Are we quick to score the seasons? "This fall isn't as pretty as the last, or as pretty as it is in the Northeast." Or, "The drought really messed up our color this year." Do we see the death first, instead of the life? Seasons don't keep a record. They don't judge. They just are. And each one has its own beauty, each one a divine brushstroke from above.

God sees the fall color as if He were wearing sepia-colored glasses.

That week made me think about how I look at things. I wonder what winter will look like. Will I see barren trees and gray skies or will I see a better canvas for freshly fallen snowflakes? And what about spring? What about my current situation? How do I view it differently than the way God sees it?

Often, when I, or someone I love, is disappointed that a prayer has seemingly gone unanswered, I respond with, "God simply sees something we cannot see." It is my feeble attempt at capturing Paul's point to the Corinthians, that there is an eternal plan, and our plan falls short of fulfilling it. Just once, wouldn't we all like a glimpse of seeing what God sees?

God has prepared something "no mind has conceived" in this life and beyond it. I don't want to have to buy pink-colored glasses in April. I'd rather take this to heart now and learn from it, so I'll be ready for the wonderful and eternal future with Him when finally we see what God sees.

> *Heavenly Father, Thank You for teaching us the extraordinary through the ordinary, like looking through cheap, sepia-colored sunglasses. Help me to trust that Your plans are what are best and that my plans aren't always going to align with them. Help me to know when I say, "God simply sees something we do not see," they are not empty words but truth rooted in Your Word. In Jesus' name we pray, amen.*

Weekly Wisdom Walk

This week, spend some time reading about the wisdom we gain from the Holy Spirit within us (2 Cor. 2:6–16). Pray for God to reveal an area of your life where you may need this wisdom or the grace to accept that which you do not understand. Are there circumstances in your current situation, which you have been quick to judge? Have you been disappointed recently? Do you long to see as God sees—to cast more clarity onto why you are experiencing a seemingly unanswered prayer? Sometimes, this can cause a rift in our intimacy with God. Try to connect with our all-knowing and all-seeing Father in a new way. Write a letter or journal entry to Him and pour out your questions and disappointments to Him. He has promised us grace and mercy. He will give it.

You're here to be light, bringing out the God-colors in the world (Matt. 5:14, THE MESSAGE).

MAPLE TREE

Salt and Light

Here's another way to put it: You're here to be light, bringing out
the God-colors in the world. God is not a secret to be kept.
—MATTHEW 5:14, THE MESSAGE

IN THE MOVIE, *As Good as it Gets*, there is a character study about three
wounded people, all trying to figure out their place in the world. Jack
Nicholson, the contentious protagonist, ultimately delivers a line to Helen
Hunt, "You make me want to be a better man." It is a powerful moment in
the film. This was a man who seemed beyond hope, but something about this
woman got to him. She radiated a quality he wanted to emulate. She illuminated something he realized was missing from his own existence. A light was
shining and a truth was revealed.

Do you know people like this woman? Do you have people in your life who
"make you want to be a better" person? I have a few friends who immediately
spring to mind. One of my friends is in the fine arts field. She is creative by
nature. We have been in a Bible study together for several years. She is able
to read a book critically. By that, I mean, she doesn't automatically agree with
everything she reads, nor does she automatically agree with the majority "takeaway" on the reading. She often has her own unique point of view. She seldom
speaks first. She is a terrific listener. Then, when asked her opinion, incredible
wisdom pours out. She challenges me by making me look at things from bright
new perspectives. I have to step out of the box and often consider the entire
world, not just my own corner of it. She is not one to offer up platitudes or
clichés either. Instead, she draws from her own rich vocabulary and comments
so profoundly I wish I could retain all she offers to ponder later. When I am not

learning from her, she encourages me. She emanates the light of Jesus in more ways than I could capture and often she doesn't even use words. She makes me want to be a better person.

I have another friend. He is a family friend, our best. He, too, seems to look at the world from a slightly different perspective than the rest of us. He just stands out—doesn't blend, in a good way! At dinnertime, he sings his prayer rather than speaks it. He is 100 percent authentic and incredibly humble. We vacation with him in the summer sometimes. One year we were playing a game with our children. First, you draw a question from a deck of cards. Then, you're required to name as many words as you can in response, using the letters of the alphabet remaining on the board. It was his turn and although "q" and "x" had somehow been used, many more difficult letters remained. His question was "What makes you angry?" Without even thinking, he replied "Hatred," "Ignorance," "Jealousy," "Racism," "Violence," "War" and won the game! Our children were watching. We were all speechless. What a godly example. He makes me want to be a better person.

As I watch fall approaching, with the long, crisp nights and the sunny, blue-sky days, I cannot help but notice the maple tree first. I love to watch how these trees change with their many hues. Sometimes, one side of the tree, the sunlit side, will turn first. Lately, as I have been watching the maple, I have thought of my friends. The light they exude reminds me of our Savior and makes me want to be more like Him. My reflection recalls the words Jesus spoke when he taught about salt and light in his Sermon on the Mount, *"You're here to be light, bringing out the God-colors in the world. God is not a secret to be kept"* (Matt. 5:14, THE MESSAGE, emphasis added). God-colors! How beautiful. That is what my friends are. That is what my friends do. They are God-colors and with their rich faith, deep thought, and refusal to look through the filter of this world, they bring out the God-colors in me and all with whom they come in contact. This is what we are all called to do. We are called to be the light that brings glory to the maple trees in our lives—those longing to be exposed to the sunbeams of our Savior.

> *Lord Jesus, we praise You for Your Word and guidance on how to live our lives and glorify You. Thank You for those You have placed in our lives as examples of what it means to be salt and light and, in return, help us to be salt and light, also, bringing out the God-colors in those we encounter each day. Give us opportunities where we might make a positive, lasting effect on someone's life. Keep our hearts, minds, and eyes focused on You so that we won't forget what You have called us*

to do and who You've called us to be. Let us not keep You a secret, but through our words and actions make You known to all who do not know Your glory and gracious love. In Your name we pray, amen.

WEEKLY WISDOM WALK

Who brings out the God-colors in you? Why not send them a little note this week or acknowledge them in some special way? Read "Jesus Teaches about Salt and Light," Matthew 5:13–16, this week. What is your "takeaway" from this reading? Have you been salt lately? Light? Has someone manifested in these ways toward you? How do we lose our saltiness or hide our light? Think of some examples and journal them. Spend some time with Jesus over the next few days with a renewed commitment to let your light shine and bring out the God-colors in those around you. Remind yourself of your commitment every time you see a maple tree!

I will forgive their sins and forget the evil things they have done (Jer. 31:34, CEV).

FORGIVE AND FORGET

Choice

I will forgive their sins and forget the evil things they have done.
—JEREMIAH 31:34, CEV

I HAVE A GREAT memory. It is both a blessing and a curse. When I was very young, my parents asked me to memorize the license plate of a speeder wreaking havoc in our neighborhood, crashing into property and dashing off without concern or conscience. Four decades later, I still remember that plate number, although it's of little use to me now. Many have compared my mind to a sponge. It continues to absorb more information. This has been a blessing on many occasions, particularly in school. It is most helpful to have almost total recall when taking an exam. The curse occurs when there are moments I'd much rather forget—arguments with people, whether it's their words or mine. I can remember virtually every word, the posturing, gestures, body language, and voice inflection. I remember circumstances as well as sights and smells. I can call them up from memory and relive it. Sometimes, it becomes a test of will and choice. Do I want to go there? I haven't always chosen the healthiest path. My choices have been in direct proportion to my spiritual growth as I have learned about forgiveness and grace.

There is an important linkage here taking a lifetime to master, however. It is the "forgetting." Often, I wish I didn't have such a great memory because of this. We have all heard people say, "Oh, I can forgive, but I will never forget!" It is a way, I think, of unwittingly tethering ourselves to something potentially destructive. We rationalize that we are holding on to it just in case we need it as some sort of protection from future attack. I admit I have been guilty of this loopy logic.

I have often wondered about God's memory. God is omniscient, all-knowing. He knows the meditations of our hearts before we ever speak them (Ps. 19:14). He knew all of our days before one of them came to be (Ps. 139:13–16). He knows when we rise and when we lie down (Ps. 139:2–3). He knows every hair on our head (Matt. 10:30). And, He knows our sin. He sent His only son to die for it (John 3:16). He keeps a book of life, a heavenly record of the faithful (Luke 10:20). Can God possibly choose to be forgetful? According to this week's scripture, I think yes!

Consider David in his lament "Wash away all my iniquity and cleanse me from my sin. For I know my transgressions, and my sin is always before me... wash me, and I will be whiter than snow" (Ps. 51:2–3, 7). Did God deliver? Yes, in fact, David received a clean slate and became the greatest king of biblical times. In 1 John we read, "Whoever does not love does not know God, because God is love." Accordingly, Paul's letter to the Corinthians, in his great passage about what love is and what it is not, he writes, love "keeps no record of wrongs." So, if God is love, then God keeps no record of wrongs?!

Wow! The God of the universe, who knows all and sees all, the One who could keep a record, indeed a book, of all our ill-fated deeds, actions, words, thoughts, and intentions chooses to wipe the slate clean, create in us a clean heart, make us white as snow... all we have to do is ask (Acts 3:19).

While taking a brisk walk in the cool fall weather, I noticed some type of feather reed grass still in bloom. This grass towers over all shrubs. A firm bushy base, allowing just enough freedom to sway with the autumn breeze, stabilizes these white, feathery plumes. Giant paintbrushes, they wafted across their canvas, a fantastic tree of crimson foliage on its last cycle before winter robbed it of its leaf life. For me, it was a metaphor for what our heavenly Father did and still does for us. He sent his only Son to die and shed His blood. "Though your sins are like scarlet, they shall be as white as snow; though they are red as crimson, they shall be like wool" (Isa. 1:18).

Father God, We praise You for Your omniscience and thank You for being a Father who chooses to both forgive and forget. Help us to follow Your example with others and with ourselves. In Jesus' name, we pray, amen.

Weekly Wisdom Walk

This week there are a lot of scripture references provided. Spend the week in the Word. Read not only the scripture but the context. Pray before your reading and ask God to reveal his truth to you. Maybe you will learn something new about the character of our Most High. Make an effort to carve out quality time and allow this week to be a time of concentrated reflection and connection between you and your Father. And, if there is anything you need to confess and ask forgiveness for, do so with a renewed understanding of just how big and gracious our God is! Have a great week.

When Jesus saw their faith, he said to the paralytic, "Son, your sins are forgiven" (Mark 2:5).

FRIENDS AND FAITH

Friendship

When Jesus saw their faith, he said to the paralytic, "Son, your sins are forgiven."
—MARK 2:5

I LOVE THE STORY of Jesus healing the paralyzed man. Little is told us about the man. The story is not as much about him. It is a story of faith—those who have big faith and those who have little. Although they were religious leaders, the Pharisees, had little faith in Jesus. In this, the beginning of the Messianic Age, they believed Him a blasphemer. The bearers of the paralytic's mat, on the other hand, had big faith. Theirs was the kind of faith, which always stopped Jesus in the middle of a talk or a walk. Imagine it! Teaching as many as could fit inside a crowded home in Capernaum, with masses swarming outside. Without given to pause, Jesus calmly wipes a little straw from His shoulders. Then, a few clumps of mud fall in His hair along with some dusty tile pieces. All eyes, once pinned on Him, begin to look up. Jesus leans back to watch the incredible act of faith play out before Him, as some men lower their paralyzed friend to His feet.

Can't you just see it? I wonder what the paralyzed man was feeling. What was he thinking on this life-changing day? Had he resigned himself to his paralytic state for the rest of his life? Was he in a place of acceptance? Was this his cockamamie friends' idea? Or, was he still very much in grief about his condition, clinging to hope that someday, someday, he would be healed—and that today was the day!

We will never know the answers to these questions, but we live through the same conundrums all the time. When our loved ones suffer, we want desperately to bring them to the feet of our Lord and Savior, the Divine Healer, and ask for complete restoration of their bodies. We ask for intervention through wise counsel and guidance through doctors' hands. We pray for God's comfort and peace. We ask for discernment, for the right words to say, for God to guide our steps as we walk with them and for His presence to be fully known. We ask for big faith—mat bearers' faith.

And, what about when it is we who are on the mat? What do we need? Where do we find hope? We find hope in Jesus! We find hope in Jesus manifest in our own mat bearers. God created man to be in community. He said it is not good for man to be alone (Gen. 2:18). We need each other. We need community. We need to bear one another's burdens; to encourage each other; to love one another; to be like Jesus to each other when our faith becomes little and we need a dose of big faith, as well as, some time spent at the feet of our Savior. We need a hole in our roof to let the sunbeams shine the healing light of Jesus on our woundedness and brokenness. When we are paralyzed by our circumstances, we will need the extra hands of our mat bearers, our friends, our family, our neighbors, our community to remove the thatch, mud, and tile separating us from the One who can restore our faith and restore our hope in Him, through which nothing is impossible.

I am reminded of this hope, restoration, and limitless possibility as I stand beneath a canopy of yellow leaves, branched out in splendor against a blue autumn sky. Save for the smallest break in its coverage, I would have been completely sheltered by the tree. Yet the opening allowed me to experience radiating warmth from the heavens above. I know, in these precious moments, God is there. Although surrounded by suffering, I glance heavenward and, suddenly, have big faith. As the writer of Hebrews pens, "Now faith is being sure of what we hope for and certain of what we do not see" (Heb. 11:1). I do not need to see God, or His feet, to know that He is there. I see Him in the yellow canopy, in the hole in its roof, and in the light shining through. Most of all, I see Him in the faith of my friends, the brave, the wounded, the broken, the grief stricken, the sick, the mourning, and the mat bearing. I am grateful to see Jesus everyday.

> *Heavenly Father, We praise You for being a Father of relationship and giving us the gift of community. Help us never to take either for granted. Create in us a desire to grow in our relationship with You and with others. Equip us with hearts for others and give us big faith, so that we may be positive examples for those around us. Give us opportunities to be mat bearers to those in need. In Jesus' name we pray, amen.*

Weekly Wisdom Walk

Read "Jesus Heals a Paralytic" (Mark 2:1–12). Who are your mat bearers? Have you carried anyone's mat recently? Are you walking with someone through a crisis, bringing them to the feet of Jesus? Being a caregiver, encourager, or mat-bearer can be exhausting work if we are not equipped by the One who can do all things! Pray before your encounters and seek out scripture to help you in your support. Remember, our faith is contagious!

"May you never bear fruit again!" Immediately the tree withered (Matt. 21:19).

FRUITFUL IMPRESSIONS

Bearing Fruit

Seeing a fig tree by the road, he went up to it but found
nothing on it except leaves. Then he said to it, "May you
never bear fruit again!" Immediately the tree withered.
—Matthew 21:19

EACH YEAR OF motherhood passes, leaving a trail of memories, lessons
learned, and moments to cherish, as well as hurdles overcome and
valleys travailed, longing to be forgotten. There are milestones, monu-
ments, markers, one and all; touch points, teaching opportunities, victories,
and failures. As I watch the seasons change, I reflect on the seasons of parenting
traveled. I remember the times, for example, when I ran interference for my son
as a toddler to keep him from harm's way and am thankful he can now make
these distinctions for himself. His curiosity is no longer peaked by poisonous
mushrooms and wild berries for birds.

Isn't it curious how we forget the fascination we had with such things until
we see them again through our own child's eyes? We, too, had to learn there
were fruit trees from which to eat and those to simply admire. Either, the fruit
wasn't pleasing or not for human consumption. Some fruit, while perfectly
appropriate to eat, became much more intriguing for play; pomegranates, for
example. While I have learned to love pomegranates as an adult, as a military
brat, they served as our grenades in childhood games of combat. My favorite
childhood fruit came from a tree that adorned the streets of my youth. Chinese
plums, we called them. To this day, I don't know their real name. We didn't
even know if they were edible, but I'm alive today to tell the tale! While I'm not

a huge fan of figs, there is nothing like the fresh variety picked straight from a tree in the backyard of a childhood friend—it makes a lasting impression.

Jesus liked figs. He was hungry one day and upon seeing a tree in full leaf, He hoped to satisfy His hunger with a fig or two. Yet, the tree bore no fruit. This was a tree that could have fed Him, but it did not offer any nourishment. So, what did He do? Find another use for it, like the pomegranate of my youth, which offered no sustenance? No, He killed the tree! Geez! Kinda harsh, don't you think? Maybe it just needed a little fertilizer or a little more time, some sunlight, perhaps. Actually, Jesus used the fruitless tree to teach his disciples about hypocrisy and guarding against the way of the Pharisees, all leaf and no fruit. The fruitless fig tree becomes a metaphor for our spiritual lives. We can do all the due diligence we want, attend church every Sunday, pray without ceasing, go to Bible Studies, practice our disciplines, but if we are not bearing fruit—what's the point? Are we not then like the hypocrites, all grand gesture and no substance... no sustenance? Jesus wants us to bear fruit "…the fruit of the Spirit is love, joy, peace, patience, kindness, goodness, faithfulness, gentleness and self-control" (Gal. 5:22–23).

To the disciples' amazement and wonder, Jesus cursed the tree and the tree immediately withered. As I watch the fall leaves wither and fall to the ground, I think of the fig tree and reflect on my childhood memories. I wonder about spiritual fruit. Unlike edible fruit, spiritual fruit isn't seasonal. While there may be a noticeable absence of plums and figs at the grocer, how accessible is my own fruit for those who hunger? Has it withered like the leaves left to be raked into a pile to burn, or is my fruit ripe and enticing, full of juice, plump for the picking? If my leaves have withered, I want to be restored by Jesus—fruitful once again. Yes, there is something about being nourished by fresh fruit. Young or old, it is a juice-dripping, sweet experience. Jesus can transform us into this kind of fruit, even if we find ourselves only in full leaf. We can go to Him and leave that lasting impression on the lives of others, like the fruit of our youth.

Gracious Lord, examine our spiritual life and show us where we need refreshment and restoration. Infuse new life into our fruit, Lord, and use us as spiritual food for all who need to be fed Your truth. Create opportunities for those we encounter to find nourishment and comfort from You when in our presence. In Your name we pray, amen.

Weekly Wisdom Walk

Read "The Fig Tree Withers" (Matt. 21:18–22). Discover what Jesus also has to say about doubt, faith, and belief in these five short verses. Take stock on these four important principles in your spiritual life this week. Ask yourself these questions regarding your own fruitfulness?

- Am I bearing spiritual fruit?

- Is there someone in my life that has come to me in need of nourishment, yet I have missed the opportunity due to withered leaves?

- Who do I go to when I need to be nourished?

- Have I been hypocritical, like a Pharisee? Ask God to search your heart on this and lead you in the way everlasting (Ps. 139:23–24).

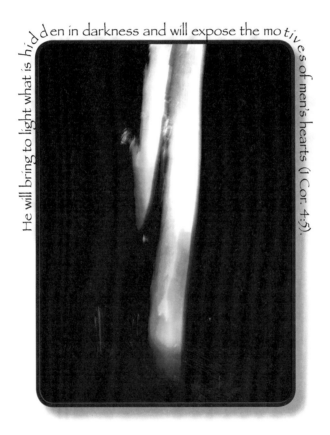

He will bring to light what is hidden in darkness and will expose the motives of men's hearts (1 Cor. 4:5).

ILLUMINATION

Judgment

Therefore judge nothing before the appointed time; wait till the Lord comes. He will bring to light what is hidden in darkness and will expose the motives of men's hearts. At that time each will receive his praise from God.
—1 CORINTHIANS 4:5

IN PHOTOGRAPHY CLASS we learned about how a camera operates. An exposure results when the right amount of light falls on an image to create a good picture. Great photography is all about the light. The faster the shutter speed, the less light passes through the aperture, or opening in the lens. By controlling the light intake, a photographer can create any number of effects. More light might be used to blur the background and sharpen a focal point image, while less light will permit a clean crispness to virtually everything captured in the frame.

It is interesting to me how we, with these instruments, have such power to manipulate what we see. With the advent of computer technology to perfect our photo flaws, we have actually turned old-school photography into a beautiful art form, practically a new field. No longer does an image have to resemble its original form, we can change it.

I started thinking about some of the terms we use in photography—dark room, overexposure, negative. The words create unrest in me out of context. How counterintuitive for a medium not intended, necessarily, to evoke such feelings. Interesting how powerful words can be.

In Paul's letter to the Corinthians, he warns about how they were using their words in judgment of him and each other regarding their faithfulness to God. "Therefore judge nothing before the appointed time; wait till the Lord comes.

He will bring to light what is hidden in darkness and will expose the motives of men's hearts. At that time each will receive his praise from God" (1 Cor. 4:5). Paul uses a metaphor of darkness and light to make a critical point. But, what I love most is how positively his words are framed.

Paul has opened his aperture wide and let the light of Jesus shine fully on his focal point so the message is crystal clear. Only God can see the motives of men's hearts. What is a blur to you and me, is a sharp image to God. And, while we may see judgment as a harsh word, here in context, Paul is saying those whose faithfulness is to be honored will receive praise from God. He will see it—the motive of the heart, which others cannot see—and He will give praise. No condemnation for a life righteously lived for Him. No negatives. We will not be overexposed, but rightly exposed.

It has been said, our eyes are like the windows to our souls. In other words, like the relationship between photographer and camera lens, we have the ability to control how much light gets in. The snapshot of our life is a reflection of the amount of light we allowed to filter through our own lens. Let us all open our eyes to the light of Jesus and allow His light to fall on the images of our life. Let us create worthy exposures for His judgment and praise. "Your eye is a lamp that provides light for your body. When your eye is good, your whole body is filled with light. But when it is bad, your body is filled with darkness. Make sure that the light you think you have is not actually darkness. If you are filled with light, with no dark corners, then your whole life will be radiant, as though a floodlight were filling you with light" (Luke 11:34–36, NLT).

> *Father of Light, shine mercifully on us and help us to step out of darkness into Your light. Search our hearts for our unfair judgments of others and expose them to Your healing rays. Open our eyes wide and illuminate the darkest recesses of our bodies, bringing out all things hidden. Help us to maintain our focus on You. In Jesus' name we pray, amen.*

WEEKLY WISDOM WALK

Why do we judge others knowing God is the only One who knows all, sees all? In 1 Samuel, no one considered David to be God's next chosen king because, "The Lord does not look at the things man looks at. Man looks at the outward appearance, but the Lord looks at the heart" (1 Sam. 16:7). We are quick to judge by earthly standards. This is what Paul was warning the Corinthians about as well. Only God can know a man's motives. Those cannot be seen. On the other hand, Jesus also talks about when it is appropriate to "judge" fellow Christians, out of love, in a way that helps them get back on the right track, but only if you have first examined yourself. In other words, this should not be done from a place of hypocrisy. Read Matthew 7:1–6 on "Judging Others" from Jesus' Sermon on the Mount. This is an often-misunderstood piece of scripture. Read any study notes you can find on this excerpt. Examine your life circumstances and see where this issue of judgment might apply to you and those close to you right now.

Therefore, as we have opportunity, let us do good to all people, especially to those who belong to the family of believers (Gal. 6:10).

Week 38

THE "SAVING" PEN

Kindness

Therefore, as we have opportunity, let us do good to all people,
especially to those who belong to the family of believers.
—GALATIANS 6:10

SITTING AT A coffee shop, nestled in my favorite leather chair by the fire-place, where I do my Bible study, I noticed a man out of the corner of my eye. With his sights pinned on the only other leather chair, staking its claim in front of the big stone hearth, he headed my direction. While juggling a cell phone on his ear, a laptop satchel, a writing tablet and, of course, a steaming cup of coffee, he pat himself down for a pen.

Without wanting to draw more attention to the gentleman, I quietly reached for the pen balancing between my lap and my book and I motioned toward him to take it, only glancing away from my book for a split second, so there was no question I fully intended for him to take it. Yet, the man motioned my gesture away.

Moments later, his phone call ended. Still juggling his paraphernalia, he finally seemed to settle himself in the big comfortable leather chair and let it envelope him in a reassuring way. Everything was starting to fall in place. Soon, his coffee had a table, his laptop had a lap, and the hearth held his satchel, but his notepad was empty. There was no pen to fill it with his insights and knowl-edge. Again, he became unsettled and restarted the ritual of patting himself down, every pocket of his clothing and every nook of his satchel feverishly investigated.

Once again, I offered my pen. He looked at me and replied, "No thank you, I need this for long term" to which, I replied, "You can have it." The gentleman looked at me quizzically. "Can I buy you a cup of coffee?" He said. "No, I have enough." I responded. He thanked me, accepted the pen, and we continued about our study, side by side. A while passed, and I had to leave. When I stood to go, the man, again on the cell phone and writing with the pen, paused in the middle of his conversation to say, "Thanks again, you saved the day!" I said, "You're welcome." However, later that day, I found myself really drawn to the words he chose. "You *saved* the day!"

How can a pen save the day? And, what is it in us that hesitates to accept a random act of kindness without thinking we must reciprocate by buying a cup of coffee in return? I think I may have felt the same way had the tables been turned. Why do we feel unworthy and feel we must repay? This is the opposite of what grace teaches us. We are all unworthy, but God, through His infinite grace loves us anyway. We cannot earn it. So, if we want to be like Jesus to others, we must love as He loves.

Paul said to the Galatians, "as we have opportunity, let us do good to all people." The following week, I was going through the drive-thru of another coffee shop. When I reached the window to pay, the attendant told me that the woman in the car in front of me had paid for my coffee and wished me a nice day! It was a neighbor. I was struck by how this random act of kindness had come full circle and now I was the receiver, rather than the giver. There was nothing I did to earn this. I learned I did not need to repay it. Yes, I could build a shallow argument for how she saved the day (it was coffee after all). But, all I really needed to do was to be gracious for godly examples.

I don't know of a pen that has the quality to save, but I know Someone who does. Jesus saved us through the cross. And, it is Jesus who tells us "in everything, do to others what you would have them do to you" (Matt. 7:12) and to "Love your neighbor as yourself" (Mark 12:31).

Lord, help me to remember Your example in my everyday walk. Help me to love like You love and to be gracious, expecting nothing in return. Show me opportunities to do good to all people so that I might glorify You and exemplify Your grace here on Earth. In Jesus' precious and Holy name, amen.

Weekly Wisdom Walk

Try some random acts of kindness this week. Paul said, "Therefore, as we have opportunity, let us do good to all people, especially to those who belong to the family of believers." It is easy to be kind to our loved ones, but what about our enemies? Jesus tells us we must love them and pray for those who persecute us (Matt 5:44). We pray as Jesus taught us to pray "... thy will be done, on earth as it is in Heaven." Spend some time this week bringing a little bit of heaven here on Earth. Show the love of Jesus to somebody for no other reason than because our Lord and Savior has asked us to do it.

Blessed are those who mourn, for they will be comforted (Matt. 5:4).

DEW DROP

Grief, Mourning

Blessed are those who mourn, for they will be comforted.
—MATTHEW 5:4

HAVE YOU EVER had a good, hard cry? One of those guttural, groaning cries that reaches to your innermost being and draws from a well of perpetual tears? You know the kind I'm talking about, head in hand—the tears come easily, slowly at first, one at a time, each one salty and wet caressing your cheek as it slides down before dropping to the floor below. All too soon, the tears gather together, attaching to each other as raindrops dripping down a windowpane, creating large pools of sorrow until your entire face is wet. Before long, the flood of tears are seeking new pathways and find them along the sinuous lines of your nostrils until a single tear clings to the tip of your nose. Then and only then, do you finally reach for the tissues. You are deeply grieving.

In Greek mythology, Niobe was considered the goddess of mourning, having lost all six of her children. Legend has it Zeus turned her to stone and the stone wept perpetually. I saw a statue of Niobe recently. It was early morning. She was a beautiful statue, appropriately adorning a cemetery. What enthralled me, however, was not the beauty of the stone nor the early fall setting, oranges and reds framing her eternal posture. It was the early light falling on a single drop of morning dew clinging to the tip of her nose. It was pure poetry in this solemn place where loved ones were placed at rest and delivered into the hands of our Lord and Savior. It stirred a feeling in me that set the tone for my entire experience there.

As I walked around, I wondered, "Who are these people? What were their lives all about? Does anyone visit them anymore?" Some of the gravesites were centuries old, so perhaps not, for many. Still, Niobe, on this day, stood over them and wept. While it's true Niobe is a statue and a myth, aren't there seasons of mourning for all of us? Times when the tears seem perpetual, as if they will never stop—the well will never run dry? We do not have to experience a loss of a loved one to enter the cemeteries of life and get in touch with our grief. We grieve losses every day and mourn them just the same, if not simply for the loss of our connection to our Father—the sin of pride and self-reliance, which leads to separation from our most precious relationship of all.

Jesus spoke of this state of mourning in The Beatitudes and called us "blessed" in the first part of Matthew 5:4, when he said, "Blessed are those who mourn, for they will be comforted." The Israelites mourned their sin, the sins of their family. They tore their clothes and put on sackcloth. We do not go through such rituals now, but one expression has remained unchanged. We can go to God with our grief. He is our comfort and Jesus promises us we will be comforted, which brings us to the second part of this powerful little scripture.

We will be comforted! That's a promise. Moreover, God will use this whole process to glorify Himself. One of my favorite verses in the Bible has become the scripture by which I have chosen to live my life: "Praise be to the God and Father of our Lord Jesus Christ, the Father of compassion and the God of all comfort, who comforts us in all our troubles, so that we can comfort those in any trouble with the comfort we ourselves have received from God" (2 Cor. 1:3–4). It is out of adversity that I came to know my Lord and Savior, *as* Savior. His comfort in times of mourning has been a blessing to me and to others, not despite my seasons of grief, but because of them.

Comforting Lord Jesus, We praise You for Your Word and Your truth, which speaks into us each and every day the comfort and life-giving strength we need to know on a deep and intimate level in order to get through the challenging days. Help us to leverage that comfort and use it to glorify You, Lord. Use us as Your hands and feet to others who are lost and brokenhearted. As You came to heal the hearts of the wounded, so do we desire to continue Your work in grateful praise for all that You have done and continue to do for an undeserving world so humbled by Your grace and unconditional love. Keep us connected to You and return us to You when we become prideful and self reliant. Amen.

Weekly Wisdom Walk

Are you grieving a loss? Maybe a lost job? An empty nester? Are you suffering an illness? Have you moved into a new home and lost relationships? Are you missing God? Grief takes on many shapes and forms. Whenever there is life change, most often, there will be grief of some sort, on some scale. You do not need to lose a loved one to experience "mourning." Or perhaps you know someone who is grieving. Read 2 Corinthians 1:3–11, "The God of all Comfort." It is chock full of encouragement for the suffering; full of hope, deliverance, patience, answered prayer, but above all it speaks of the Father of all compassion who "comforts us!" He is all we need.

Fall/Winter

Here I am! I stand at the door and knock (Rev. 3:20).

THE PINECONE

Time with Jesus

Here I am! I stand at the door and knock.
—REVELATION 3:20

IT WAS FALL at the monastery. I make an annual pilgrimage there for a silent weekend retreat. Usually, I will choose a time of year when something lays heavily on my heart. This particular year it wasn't a worldly problem but a spiritual one. I had been wandering in my own personal desert, disconnected from God, despite my futile attempts through prayer to commune with Him. I had hoped some uninterrupted time at the monastery, in silence and solitude, would bring about a reconnection.

This monastery is set on many acres of picturesque Georgia woodlands, complete with wildlife, lakes, bridges, old mills and sundry other buildings the monks use to create their wares. At Friday sunset, I strolled down to the water's edge of one of the lakes. I found a bench, sat, and began to pray. I started with confession. I knew I had to become cleansed before I could, again, experience the fullness of His glory. Pride, indifference, self-involvement, duplicity—the greater the distance I had felt from God, the greater I had fallen. "You know my folly, O God; my guilt is not hidden from you" (Ps. 69:5). I prayed the scripture back to Him and soon, my prayer became a monologue of exasperation with myself and this disconnect with our Savior. "Where are you, Lord?!"

At that moment, with missile-like speed, a pinecone came crashing down, from one of the hundred-foot pine trees surrounding me, missing my head by a fraction and landing, with a *thud*, squarely on the park bench beside me. Instantaneously, the scripture from Revelation came to me as if Jesus himself were answering my question directly, "Here I am! I stand at the door and knock!" Dismissing the frolicking squirrel messengers with laser projection accuracy, this felt like the first direct answer I had received from the Lord in far too long, yet it made perfect sense. At that point in our lives, we were straddling two different churches and feeling a bit hypocritical—devoted and loyal to one, yet feeling called to another. We professed one commitment, but acted out another. Our faith in Jesus stood resolute, but our authenticity and execution in our religious alliances begged questioning.

The next day, the retreatants were invited to meet with one of the lay Cistercians for counsel. Never having broken my silence before, I felt a pull to go to her. The office was right across the hall from my room. I could slip over quietly and back again, if I lost my nerve. At the first opportunity, I took a peek. She was sitting quietly, alone on a chair in a small room. The door was open. I knocked lightly. She did not hear me or see me. I knocked again, and she invited me in. We spoke a little bit about my situation. She shared her wisdom with me and explained how these periods of wandering in the desert can be times of tremendous growth. I shared my experience down by the lake in great detail—the lake, the setting sun, the playful squirrels, various other wildlife and, of course, the pinecone. She listened intently, suggesting that I may have already established my reconnection. "Well, it was a knock," I replied. We spent about an hour together. When I got up to leave, I noticed a cross on the floor. This time, I didn't hear the "thud." I only saw the cross. I motioned to it, but she didn't respond. I reached down to pick it up and offered it, "Someone must have dropped this cross." It was hers. Like the pinecone, it had fallen, but silently.

Later that day, after I had time to absorb all of her wise counsel and allow it to resonate deep in my soul, I watched someone walk with her back to her room. It was then, the scales were removed from my eyes and tears quickly filled them. She was blind. How arrogant I felt. I came here wanting, wanting, wanting. Now, I found myself ungrateful for something I already possessed— the simplest of gifts—for sight. Only hours before, I had blathered on and on about the many sights I had seen by the lake and the numerous visual ways I experience God in creation. So shackled by self-pity and pride, I couldn't see the obvious signs, which lay before me. This wise woman couldn't see me at her door, because she lost the gift of her sight. She could not see that her cross had dropped to the floor because she was blind. Yet, she listened intently to my descriptive visualization of the lake scene, because although she had lost her sight, she was fascinated by mine and never hesitated throughout my story to remind me how much God loves me. She had not lost sight of the most precious gift of all. God is here. God has said, "Never will I leave you; never will I forsake you" (Heb. 13:5). God used a blind woman to help me see.

The falling of a simple pinecone set much in motion for me on this fall weekend: Two objects fell—the pinecone and the cross. Two doors were encountered—one door was closed and required a knock, the other door was open. One woman could see, yet she was blind. The other, blind, yet she could see.

> *Precious Lord, thank You for Your promise never to leave us. Thank You for Your unconditional love. Even when You seem distant, help me always to remember that You are near. Thank You for Your forgiveness and for closing my eyes, so that I might see You more clearly. And, most of all thank You for Your special messengers, the whimsical and the wise. In Jesus' name, amen.*

WEEKLY WISDOM WALK

Has it been awhile since you really connected with God? Consider going on retreat. There are many retreat centers available for daily or overnight stays. Silence and solitude are just two of the spiritual disciplines, which can enrich your prayer life and bring you into a deeper, more intimate fellowship with our Creator. If you love the outdoors, choose a facility with breathtaking views and nature trails. Saturate yourself in His creation. For those who experience God through music, bring along your favorite worship songs, or pick a location that offers worship services. Bring your Bible. Immerse yourself in His Word. "My Presence will go with you, and I will give you rest" (Exod. 33:14). Schedule some silence and solitude this week, either for a half-day, full day or a weekend. Put it on your calendar: "Time with God."

Your word *is* a lamp to my feet and a light for my pa*th* (Ps. 119:105).

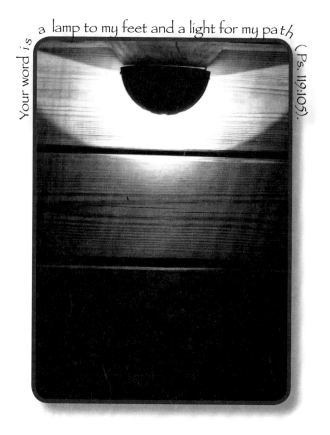

LAMPLIGHT

His Word

Your word is a lamp to my feet and a light for my path.
—Psalm 119:105

WHEN I WAS in college for the third time (yes, there is a twelve-year undergraduate plan), I was studying Interior Design. Many classes were shared by interior design, architecture, and construction management majors. One of my favorites among these courses was lighting design. Being a math geek, I loved all of the mathematics involved with lighting. One of the reasons I changed majors so often is because it took me so long to realize that while I could handle the worlds of arithmetic and science, my passion was in the creative arts. The school of architecture ultimately provided the happy medium, but lighting design was bathed in calculations. For me, it had it all!

I think this meticulous pencil gymnastics of configuring footcandles, lumens, and efficacies to create the ideal illumination for a brighter world is potentially lost on most patrons, though. But, that is precisely the point. The eye is not to be led to the lighting element but to that which is being illuminated, otherwise, the fixture has stolen the show. When walking into an art gallery, for example, no one wants to see the lighting but the masterpieces displayed. Likewise, when meandering through a beautiful garden at night, it's the new essence this botanical setting takes in the evening hours, which lies center stage to the flood of light honoring her.

Now, have you ever tried to walk around a house or a garden at night without proper lighting? Or, worse yet, no lighting, like when there is a power outage—maybe with a flashlight or candle in hand? It humors me to say, while

I have a degree in interior design, if it wasn't for the fifty-cent nightlight in the hall between our foyer and kitchen, I would stub my toe every time I made a late night run for something cool to drink! And, forget about our landscape. Our yard is treacherous after sundown. We do have some lighting, but I don't believe there were any extensive calculations made when determining where to place the lamplights. Your shoes must be practically underneath them in order to see where you are going.

Last night, as I watched the late summer sunset, the walkway lights barely illuminated my path, allowing me to follow my way back to the house. The lanterns cast only enough light to brighten a step's distance for me to walk. It reminded me of the Psalmist words, "Your word is a lamp to my feet and a light for my path" (Ps. 119:105).

Where do we go, when we need guidance or need to know our next step to take? God's Word! He has given us His truth in His Word. It is a rulebook to follow for our life, whether our road is easy or difficult, light or dark. In Biblical times, there were no streetlights strung together by electrical wires. Lanterns were a necessity. They were carried. How far do lanterns cast their ray of light? Like a lighthouse beacon, so all could see any thieves or bandits or wild prey ahead on the dirt roads traveled? No. They only illuminated the next step. The lamplight fell to the ground and bathed the path directly in front, in a flood of light, to guide the next step. The rest required faith and trust.

And, so it is with God. His Word is a lamp unto our feet illuminating our next step in life, providing the guidance we need to make all of our decisions. He has given us His commands for how to live righteously and honorably— how to love and obey, trust, serve, be faithful, respectful and humble, merciful, gracious, and forgiving. It is all in His Word. We don't require fancy lighting, just a book—His book … His Word.

> *Father God, thank You for Your Word. Thank You for giving us all we need in writing so we can live full and abundant lives as You have designed it. Help us to cling to Your Word and renew our thirst for it each day. Create in us a yearning to spend time with You every day and to apply Your Word and Your truth in our daily walk. In Jesus' name we pray, amen.*

Weekly Wisdom Walk

This week's verse is taken from the longest Psalm, and longest chapter in the Bible, Psalm 119. Read it this week. The author is unknown, but you will quickly learn of the psalmist's devotion to God's Word and His laws. Obedience to His Word is the prescription to happiness. Treat yourself. Bathe in the light of God's Word through this amazing acrostic poem (based on the letters of the Hebrew alphabet.)

And God is faithful, he will not let you be tempted beyond what you can bear (1 Cor. 10:13)

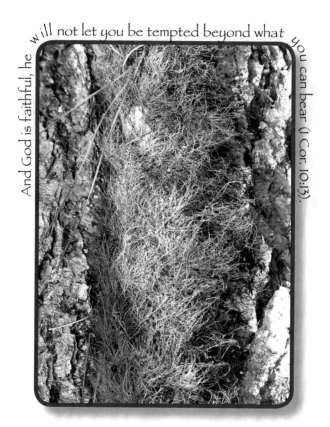

THE VINE THAT ATE THE SOUTH

Temptation

And God is faithful; he will not let you be tempted beyond
what you can bear. But when you are tempted, he will also
provide a way out so that you can stand up under it.
—1 Corinthians 10:13

HAVE YOU EVER heard the expression, "God will not give you more than you can bear?" Have you ever found yourself carrying an enormous burden and questioning God's judgment about this very issue? I have. In fact, I have scoured the Bible and I believe I have found an answer. God never made this promise! Life happens, and God has promised us His grace and mercy, when it does. How could we bear the loss of a child, the ravages of war, rape, life-threatening illnesses, senseless crimes, and a host of other heinous travesties? How could our loving Lord expect us to bear such circumstances? He would not. He would want us to lean on him. We need a mighty and compassionate God in times such as these, precisely because they *are* too much for us to bear alone.

So, what does the Bible promise, regarding this "bearing?" Where did we get tangled up? In the vine! No, not "the" vine, our God, but a much more insidious vine—the vine that ate the South. Have you ever seen it? Kudzu, it is called. To me, it is the vine of temptation. It's beautiful at first glance, blanketing everything from trees to barns with an apron of flowering foliage. It is the first to bloom in summer and the last to leave the party. I adore it. Still, temptation's story is never resigned to surface prose. There is something deeper. It is requiring. Its yield is overwhelming, growing a foot a day. Eventually, it will snuff the life out of the trees it covers by cutting off sun exposure. It is a deceptive vine, a pest.

Once summer passes and the last of the Kudzu has gone dormant, not dead mind you, but just asleep, you will find the graying branches hanging everywhere. All too quickly, you will see the burdens too great for the trees to bear, yet they have, year after year. Carrying the blanketed vines in silence, fighting for their very survival, hoping beyond hope for the weight to become lighter, something that they can bear.

So much like temptation—it looks desirable on the surface. But, once temptation has taken root, the true nature of the vine is exposed. We fool ourselves, "What's the harm?" It's just a bit of fun—playful, harmless. But, that from which God will not let you be tempted, presents a choice. Paul wrote to the Corinthians, "And God is faithful; he will not let you be tempted beyond what you can bear. But when you are tempted, he will also provide a way out so that you can stand up under it" (1 Cor. 10:13). God will provide us a way out from temptation, but sin is the evil one's playground. Should we not choose to take God's hand, we have ventured into sin. God will deliver us from temptation and will give us no more than we can bear, but the choice is ours. He won't make it for us.

As I was walking along the banks of the Chattahoochee River this fall, I saw the base of a Kudzu vine, literally, attached to an enormous tree. This tree must have been one hundred years old. The Kudzu, like a parasite, was attached to it. In the dormancy of the season, I could see the vine for what it was, without its summer masking. It was a hairy vine of gray and brown, both ugly and beautiful at the same time. Like temptation itself, the allure drew me to it. Most incredible to me was how majestic the tree looked. How the tree "stood up under it" as Paul writes, unaffected by the seductions of the vine.

God didn't promise we would meet with unbearable circumstances. I imagine there is much we will be unable to bear. That is when we will be presented with a choice. Choose God or not. God or self? When circumstances are beyond what we can bear and we do not choose God, we often choose self—self-loathing, self-medication, self-mutilation, self-pity, selfishness—the list is daunting. What God promised us is our *reaction* to circumstances. These temptations, which entice us to "dull" the pain, will be bearable and He will provide the way out, so that we can stand up under it, like the tree.

> *Abba, we praise You for Your compassion. Thank You for being a Father of relationship so that we might have a place to go when we meet with circumstances and temptations beyond which we can bear. Call us to You in those moments of weakness and remind us that You are the only one with the power to sustain us through such darkness.*

Give us the strength to stand up under it. In Jesus' name we pray, amen.

Weekly Wisdom Walk

Are you bearing a heavy burden? Are you tempted to handle the situation by your own power? Identify, confess, and surrender your temptations this week. Lean hard into our Savior. He has promised to deliver you and provide you a way out.

Look at the birds of the air...your heavenly Father feeds them. Are you not much more valuable than they? (Matt. 6:26).

SOUTHBOUND FLIGHT

Worry

Look at the birds of the air; they do not sow or reap or store away in barns,
and yet your heavenly Father feeds them. Are you not much more valuable
than they? Can any one of you by worrying add a single hour to your life?
—MATTHEW 6:26–27

BEFORE I BECAME a professing Christian, I was a chronic worrier. In fact,
I still worry on occasion, but my worry now, pales in comparison to
my worry then. At times I wished there were a twelve-step program for
what my mother called "worry warts." She was a worrier as well. I do not know
if she modeled the behavior, if this is something you can inherit or if tragic
circumstances at a young age predisposed me to choose worry over rational
thought. Life seemed to teach me early to expect evil to be the victor.

As years passed, I found myself worrying about everything and nothing.
If others didn't censor me from sensationalized television programs, I had
to boycott them myself. Either I would discover a new health crisis; become
quite convinced I'd been exposed and possibly symptomatic, or the plight of a
suffering world would speak to my own brokenness and fully healed old wounds
would reopen. I couldn't seem to exist desensitized to the world around me.
Quite the contrary, I over identified with it. I was of it. I was in it. And it was
swallowing me whole.

I worried every day, about everything. No one knew this pain. Therefore,
no one ran their speech through a filter before speaking to me. I tried to avoid
alarmists, pessimists, and negative thinkers at all costs. But, even the best-laid
plans are thwarted.

I was at a conference one winter's day, in upstate New York, with a bit of a sinus issue brewing. It was bitter cold—sleet, snow, the works. One misstep later and I was lying on a sheet of black ice. Cold and wet, chilled to the bone, I walked to my meeting and endured the rest of the day. By nightfall, I had a serious head cold. The next day, I was taking a southbound flight to Texas, thrilled to be going home with thoughts of curling up in my bed and pulling out all the sure-fire home remedies to ease my agony. Then, someone said it. "You know, flying is the worst thing you can do with a head cold like that. The take off and landing are going to be terrible!" I had flown a lot, but until then, I hadn't really thought about it. My worry muscle began to constrict. Moreover, it was on this trip I learned the difference between a direct flight and a non-stop flight. A direct flight goes directly to its destination, except it makes a stop or two along the way. In other words, more than one take off and landing! Yes! I was on a direct flight—my first and last!

I worried all night about this flight as my sinuses filled up and I lost my hearing in both ears. I boarded the plane with trepidation, never before having a fear of flying. As the plane began its ascent, excruciating pain began in my ears. I could not equalize them. Tears ran down my cheeks. The flight attendants were great. Soon, all of them were attending to me. I had warm compresses inside coffee cups covering both ears throughout both descents and takeoffs. Looking somewhat like a woeful Princess Leah, I endured hours of this. One eardrum burst. The other had to be lanced in the emergency room upon arrival.

The cups of comfort did nothing, yet the attention afforded me did make me feel less alone in my anguish and pain. Even though I did not know Jesus, I believe I was surrounded by some who may have. Yet, worrying did not add a single hour to my life (Matt. 6:26). In fact, on that day, it felt like it depleted it, at least the quality of it.

It is winter again. Now, I am thankful to know Jesus and to have a personal relationship with Him. While I may still worry from time to time, I am reminded of how far I have come when I witness another southbound flight—the birds that adorn our skies in Georgia. I watch them eat the winter berries on the only remaining shrubs to flower. I awake to their happy songs, traveling melodiously through the crisp morning air. God made them all, without worry. They instinctively know where to go to find food in the winter and shelter for their young. They know their Maker, too, and we are much more valuable to God than they.

There is no twelve-step program for the worrier. There is only one—the One.

Gracious Lord, thank You for Your relevant teaching about worry. It is something with which each of us struggles at some point in our lives. Help us to be mindful of when we are leaning on our own thoughts of controlling outcomes instead of Your power and sovereignty over all things. Give us the wisdom and discernment to do whatever we can to take necessary action in our lives and know when to do so, but when the rest is up to You, help us to surrender to Your will and relieve us of our inclinations to worry. In Your name we pray, amen.

Weekly Wisdom Walk

Read what Jesus tells us about worry in Matthew 6:25–34. If you have read this before, try to reread it with fresh eyes. Ask yourself, "What am I worrying about right now? What do I tend to worry about most? Why?" Have you surrendered these things to Christ? Do you do so regularly? If you are a chronic worrier, why hasn't surrender been working for you? If you have a spiritual mentor, friend, or spouse who is not a worrier, use this week as an opportunity to discuss what they do when it comes to worry and faith. If you are not a worrier, pray for God to use you to be that person for someone who is.

There is no fear in love. But perfect love drives out fear (1 John 4:18).

NO FEAR

Fear

There is no fear in love. But perfect love drives out fear, because fear has
to do with punishment. The one who fears is not made perfect in love.
—I JOHN 4:18

I FIRST MET HER during an outreach for new Christian women and seekers
in Capljina, Bosnia. It was a jewelry-making event. I knew little about
creating these artful trinkets. This was more of a time of fellowship and
connection, an opportunity to share the love of Jesus with women who may not
receive a daily dose in this mostly Muslim country, where religious freedom is
as foreign as the land we found ourselves in.

Neither of us could understand a word each other spoke, yet somehow we
managed to communicate with a woman's tendency to speak with flailing arm
gestures. Immediately, I could tell she was a woman who knew what she wanted.
She cared little whether her necklace of various sizes and shapes had perfect
symmetry, only that the black shimmering colors matched; or whether there
was slack in her bracelet, as long as everything was included as she created it.
There was a contentedness about her. She gave up on perfection long ago. It was
not important to her. She had found something more important. Tonight was
about joy. Her expectations were clear.

Had I spoken the language, I am certain I would have had a few questions
for her, but the evening was fast paced, and there was not much time to unpack
this peace she emanated. There were others more concerned about their baubles
and beads than she. Nevertheless, she left an impression on me.

Later in the week, my group would make a trip to a village for visitations
to those in need of prayer. Our last stop was to the business of a fairly new

Christian woman under extreme persecution for her new found Christian faith. It was my jewelry partner. She greeted me with a big hug and kiss for both cheeks as is customary in this country. Inside her shop, we would hear her story, which would cast a beacon of light on all of the unanswered questions raised the night of our women's outreach.

She came to have a personal relationship with Jesus Christ much to the opposition of her entire family. This is not uncommon in this region. Her father, husband, and child are opposed to her decision. She has been threatened with imprisonment and even death, by a loved one. When asked what we could pray for on her behalf, she asked if we could pray for the safety of her business and for the salvation of her family. Afterward, she openly solicited questions. Many were asked. I was having a difficult time wrapping my mind around a family member who wanted her in prison, or worse yet, dead! Despite my own childhood wounds, this was unimaginable. Still, she was beyond forgiveness, beyond grace, there was something more. It was the same contentedness I saw the night of the outreach, the peace. What was that? How did she get it? So, I asked her, "Do you ever feel in danger or threatened? Are you afraid for your life?" To this she replied (through a translator), with this same peace and utter confidence, "No, not at all. I would go through all of this again, if the alternative meant not having Jesus in my life." I realized I was standing before someone who truly loved the Lord with a perfect love.

John tells us about this truth, about the incompatibility of love and fear, "There is no fear in love. But perfect love drives out fear" (1 John 4:18). I think I finally understood how short I fall in the fear-based life I lead. My fear of the unknown, my anxieties and my worries, the "what-ifs," the "things are going too well, it must be my turn next!" Have you ever had these thoughts? This woman has known worse things and still loves Jesus for what He is going to do next. I have seen Jesus do great things in my life and fear the table is going to turn as I watch the tragedies surrounding me. Her reality is, the trinket is perfect in its imperfection. She sees herself and others as God sees her, which affords her perfect love, no fear.

We could all heed a lesson from my new friend's *pearls* of wisdom. Whether strung together or gazed upon in isolation, her message hangs together, timeless and relevant, and as brilliant as the black beads she hand selected of every shape and size to create her masterpiece, just as God created her.

Almighty God, we praise You for being sovereign over all people and all the lands. We praise You for all You have done and all You are going to do. Forgive us for our shortcomings and our doubts. We believe You are all-knowing and all-powerful. Thank You for amazing witnesses who show us, not with words, but with actions and with truth, that You are the Lord of All, so that we, too, may learn to love You with a perfect love. In Jesus' precious name we pray, amen.

WEEKLY WISDOM WALK

Do you become fearful easily? Don't be too quick to answer this question. Do you worry about providing for your family? Security? Safety? Do you have control issues? Most people can at least answer one of those positively. The truth is there is no security in this life, and we are never in control. Many of us, without even knowing it, live a fear-based life. You do not have to worry to the extremes offered in this devotion, as I served myself up on a platter, to fall into the enemy's grip! This week, journal some of the things you fear, no matter how subtle. You may surprise yourself about how pervasive they have been in your daily life. Then, spend some time walking through scripture about what you have written. Finally, surrender these things to our Sovereign God who will take them from you. Find your freedom in Him. Have a great week!

Do not cause anyone to stumble, whether Jews, Greeks or the church of God (1 Cor. 10:32).

ENGRAFTED BRANCHES

Christianity

Do not cause anyone to stumble, whether Jews, Greeks or the church of God.
—1 CORINTHIANS 10:32

EVERY ONCE IN a while I am presented with the question, "What does it mean to be a Christian?" Sometimes posed by a new Christian or a seeker, I pray for God to give me the right words to sum up all it means to be a follower of our Lord Jesus. Better on paper than the spoken word, I find myself trying to give a brief synopsis of the Bible, God's love letter to us all—an incredible and simple story, really, of God's love, patience, and faithfulness for His children. Yet, it never comes out quite that way—simple, I mean. The eyes stare back at me, glazed-over and wanting. I could recite the Apostles' Creed, the basic tenants of Christianity, or boil everything down to the minimalist's viewpoint of relationship over religion. Still, somehow, for those who have not yet experienced bathing in God's presence, knowing unequivocally, He is but a breath away whispering as a Father to child, the relationship explanation is difficult to fathom.

Most interesting to me is how heated a conversation can get when attempting to unpack this question with fellow Christians. I wonder why we cannot agree on what it means to be followers of Christ. This cannot set a very good example for the seekers out there. Often these conversations can leave you feeling isolated, frustrated, confused, and perhaps pondering Christendom altogether. In your own attempt to find out who is "right," you may scour over scripture, pray, seek counsel, in an attempt to answer the question for yourself. Indeed, "Who are we in Christ? What *does* it mean to be a Christian? Gracious Father, after all this arguing and discord, *this* cannot be it."

Before long, you feel trapped in a crisis of faith—not so much in your faith in Jesus, but in others, in your religion, in Christianity. You find yourself stumbling. Paul wrote to the Corinthians, "Do not cause anyone to stumble…" It is the ultimate depiction of doing all things to the glory of God and in so doing, to love God and love others. James later speaks of the power of the tongue and our need to tame it, "We all stumble in many ways. If anyone is never at fault in what he says, he is a perfect man, able to keep his whole body in check" (James 3:2). He recognizes we would have to be perfect if we never misspoke, since the tongue is the most difficult part of the body to tame. "With the tongue we praise our Lord and Father, and with it we curse men, who have been made in God's likeness. Out of the same mouth comes praise and cursing. My brothers, this should not be" (James 3:9–10). In Paul's letter to the Romans, a culture of Gentiles who became followers of our Savior without ever hearing testimony, never having opportunity yet to meet with Paul, but only hearing of Jesus, the resurrected Messiah and believing He was the Son of God, Paul writes, "Did they [the Israelites] stumble so as to fall beyond recovery? Not at all!" (Romans 11:11.) God is a gracious God, and not only were the Israelites capable of being grafted back in, but there was room for the Romans as well. We are all grafted in, by grace. "For it is by grace you have been saved, through faith—and this is not from yourselves, it is the gift of God—not by works, so that no one can boast" (Eph. 2:8–9).

The answer to the question, "Who are we as Christians?" We are those who believe Jesus Christ died so that we may live. We follow Him, not a religion. We have faith in Him, not in people. We love God and love others as Jesus commanded, and everything we do must be to the glory of God. And, who wouldn't want to, if not out of sheer gratitude alone, for such a gracious gift? Loving God is easy, yet loving others gets messy! What does it mean to be a Christian? This *is* it! It is easy (loving God) and it is difficult (loving others). Sometimes it takes work. "If all you do is love the lovable, do you expect a bonus? Anybody can do that" (Matt. 5:46, THE MESSAGE).

We need a very big and sovereign God—a God of relationship, who we can come before every day—in order to fulfill the tall order of loving Him, loving others, and doing it all to the glory of God. To be a follower means not just to believe but to put into daily practice the Word of God and the teachings of Christ Jesus, knowing we are not perfect, "for all have sinned and fall short of the glory of God" (Rom. 3:23). It may sound simple, but it isn't. Not as long as we have worldly thoughts to guide runaway tongues. Not as long as there are believers and unbelievers confronting us with difficult or challenging questions and loving us with conditional love. For this, and so much more, we need an all-powerful, all-knowing, gracious Father, who loves us unconditionally. Fortunately, our engrafted branches are rooted in One.

Faithful Father, we give thanks for Your patience with us. Help us keep our thoughts focused on You. Lord, especially when challenged, give us self-control, particularly with our tongues. Let us honor You with our words. Help us to choose rightly. Use us to bring Your kingdom here on Earth. Help us to abide in You and Your Word each day. Give us immeasurable love and patience with others. In Your name we pray, amen.

WEEKLY WISDOM WALK

This week, use your concordance or computer word search to find relevant scriptures regarding today's reading. Try searching on "stumble" and "word" or "words," The Bible has much to say about the power in our words. Choose a few that speak to you personally and make a bookmark out of them or place them in a conspicuous place. Make sure to read them in full context. Then, memorize the verses and ponder them in your heart this week. Be conscious of your words this week and reflect on your words lately. Have you caused another to stumble? Has someone caused you to stumble either recently or in your past? Bring your concerns to your Father in Heaven.

Like clouds and wind without rain is a man who boasts of gifts he does not give (Prov. 25:14).

UNCLEAVING

Discord in Marriage

Like clouds and wind without rain is a man
who boasts of gifts he does not give.
—PROVERBS 25:14

TWO DECADES. MANY of my friends never believed my marriage would last more than six months. My husband and I were from different worlds. We were vastly different people. We barely knew each other when we promised ourselves to cleave to one another for all eternity. It is said, "opposites attract." No truer statement could be made to sum up our reality physically, emotionally, and spiritually. Inside and out, we were different. Psychologists would say we shouldn't have lasted as long as we have. It "should" have ended shortly after the newness wore off, once the novelty faded, the flame smoldered to mere glowing embers. But, it did last.

We were drawn to each other by the flame and the magnificent light. Like magnets, it was the differences that attracted us. Often, in marriage, we might see couples beginning to look like each other, and their dog! These are probably the marriages that are "supposed" to work because there aren't so many differences and hurdles to overcome. They have more in common, similar interests and backgrounds. Make no mistake, being complete opposites is no picnic, but the real gift is in learning to embrace the differences as gifts the other brings to the relationship.

After twenty years, it is quite easy to look back and notice somewhere, at least some of them, ceased bringing life to the relationship with their gift-giving qualities and became rubs, qualities that annoy rather than add to the relationship. When we see this dynamic occur, we realize what we loved and

189

appreciated about each other has become the very thing we are allowing to uncleave us, a vow we made before God. We desperately pour into our woundedness and pray through our pride. Because, pride is what it is. We are boasting on some level that our way is the right way, spontaneity over planning, rationality over dreaming, logic over emotion, head over heart, work over play.

Neither is correct, of course. We lose perspective. We lose sight of the gifts we brought to the marriage and those we value in the other. In doing so, we fail to acknowledge the worth of our spouse. Everyone wants to be loved, to be heard, and to be valued. In recognizing, embracing, and honoring each other's differences, we honor the person and give them great value. When we do not, the emotion manifested is one of worthlessness.

The region in which we live has been in a drought for several years. We are finally beginning to see rain clouds on a regular basis. Still, all too familiar are those clouds which fill the heavens giving great assurances our parched land will be gifted with revitalizing rains, but sometimes the promise is an empty one. The clouds pass us by and we feel defeated and discouraged, still thirsty and in need of nourishment. Our marriages are the same. We need not boast of our gifts or claim to be right, presenting our well-articulated arguments of how much more sense it makes to be practical versus whimsical. We need only to remind ourselves of the time when the very points we were making were not issues of division, but the very gifts binding our hearts together. Celebrate them. Embrace them and remember the value they once held. We can give them as gifts again.

> Like clouds and wind without rain is a man who boasts of gifts he does not give.
>
> —PROVERBS 25:14

Heavenly Father, we praise You for creating marriage and thank You for the privilege when we have been chosen to share our life with another. Help us to always remember this incredible honor and the vows we made before You to uphold the promises from Your Word. Guard our thoughts and our tongue and let us cherish the gifts we each bring to this relationship bound in Your love. Let us give lavishly to the ones we have chosen to partner with in life. In Jesus' name, amen.

Weekly Wisdom Walk

Are you married? If not, you know someone who is. Embracing differences is just one in a long list of secrets to a successful marriage. My husband and I will often take a pulse on our marriage when it feels like we are not "in sync." Many times, we will notice the issue has been undergirding our daily life for longer than we expected. Where did the wheel fall off the wagon? Only through unpacking the day-to-day dynamics through conversation will we discover patterns and problems, seemingly small and not worth mentioning. Yet, it is the little things that pile up and become big, leading to resentment. Tracing them back to a pivotal point in the relationship may reveal a time when we stopped valuing one another. A small life change or event may have caused a ripple effect, but left us unaware of the source. And so our gifts became burdens and our way became the only way. He was unmoving and she was insensitive. The clouds rolled along without quenching our thirst, yet we got stuck, spun our wheels and created the illusion we moved along undisturbed by the winds of change. If you are married, take your "pulse" this week. Use biblical references to help you either get back on or stay on the path of marital health anointed in God's blessings. "A cord of three strands is not quickly broken" (Eccles. 4:12). Do not forget the third strand in our marriages is God, Who has woven us together and united us as one.

We take captive every thought to make it obedient to Christ (2 Cor. 10:5).

CHATTERBOX

Thought Life

> We demolish arguments and every pretension that sets
> itself up against the knowledge of God, and we take captive
> every thought to make it obedient to Christ.
> —2 CORINTHIANS 10:5

A S A CHILD of the Sixties, I was fortunate to be among those who received the first talking doll. You remember the pull-string in the back. The first mechanized version of what is now a dinosaur in the world of technology toys. Her name was "Chatty Cathy" and as her name implies, she was a talker, just like me. The world marveled at how this little one could be such a chatterbox. We were a perfect pair. It wasn't long before my family nicknamed me Chatty Kathy, the only differences between us being how we spelled our names and, of course, all of that vinyl for skin.

Fast-forward almost fifty years and I have no idea what ever came of my doll, yet I am still quite chatty. In fact, I have wondered, "Have I ever had an unexpressed thought?" Sadly, I believe the answer is, "No." If not for the fact I have pondered this question and have now asked it and answered it, the answer is most definitely, "No!"

Thought is the seed to the spoken word. Yet as fast as my mind races through them, my mouth manages to keep a step ahead. I love to engage others in intellectual conversation. Sometimes, I deflect uncomfortable ones with humor. I have discovered the power of words, but the result is not always pleasant or positive. Why? Because the seed, the thought that precedes the word, must be tested, watered, nourished, and nurtured, before it is ready to break through the earth and be shared for another to receive benefit.

How often do we carefully consider our words from their infancy as mere thoughts? Instead, many of us can be careless with them. I am the greatest offender.

Paul instructs us in 2 Corinthians 10:5, "We demolish arguments and every pretension that sets itself up against the knowledge of God, and we take captive every thought to make it obedient to Christ." I love to picture capturing thoughts before they escape my mouth, then examining them, one by one; testing them against the wisdom and knowledge we have received from the Holy One. How many prideful disputes could be abated, how many unnecessary confrontations? Our need to be right could be replaced by a longing to be righteous and obedient. "Those who have knowledge use words with restraint" (Prov. 17:27).

The Bible tells us, "Before a word is on my tongue you, Lord, know it completely" (Ps. 139:4). Christ knows my every movement, the meditations of my heart, before I even speak them, the good and the bad. Just knowing Christ is so intimately aware of my thought life should give me pause and allow me to control my tongue. But, I am flesh. My thoughts are not like His thoughts. His thoughts, His ways are higher. When I was a child, I talked like a child. I thought like a child. I reasoned like a child. I am no longer a child. The toys today are interactive to the point of appearing to "think" before responding to a whirlwind of information.

As I watch the fall leaves, products of what were once seeds, caught up in a wind tunnel, twirling about like a funnel cloud of dancing color, I imagine each one a thought. I notice a line of moss-covered cinderblocks catching those escaping the breezy activity. Each cell fills with the autumn debris set free from perpetual circulation. Such is the swirl of thoughts in my head. My prayer is for the freedom to have flowing thought, but the discipline to capture each one and sit with it for however long it takes, until it is obedient to Christ Jesus—even if it means allowing a little moss to grow on it before releasing it into spoken word.

Merciful Father, thank You for Your wise instruction about our words and thoughts. We praise You for the way You love us. You are all-knowing and all-seeing. Nothing is hidden from You. Help us to be as transparent with others, yet soften our speech and delivery so that our words match the unwavering love of Christ we are called to have for each other, and give us the ability to love so deeply. Create in us such Christlike authenticity that capturing our thoughts will become automatic and our words will reflect the glory of Your Son Jesus. It is in His name we pray, amen.

Weekly Wisdom Walk

Have you ever found yourself in a conversation, realizing there is no turning back? Maybe you did not think it through before you started talking? Perhaps, the subject was divorce and suddenly you realized someone in the room is facing one. Consider the times this may have happened to you. Jot them down, and then read through as many relevant scriptures as you can find pertaining to "thought." Find a key verse that resonates with you. Commit it to memory this week.

Out of the same mouth come praise and cursing. My brothers and sisters, this should not be (James 3:10).

A FRAGILE CHOICE

Words, Attitude

Out of the same mouth come praise and cursing.
My brothers, this should not be.
—JAMES 3:10

MY HUSBAND IS a self-proclaimed procrastinator. I can claim it, because he has already confessed it. He is not ashamed of it, and to be honest, it often works out in his favor. If he has failed to fertilize the lawn, for example, he will wait until the last day only to notice a rain cloud waiting to set the chemicals for him. He has somehow managed to meet the deadline and save our water bill all at the same time.

Christmas shopping is another arena, which boggles my mind each year. How he manages to cover his list in one day, Christmas Eve, I will never quite comprehend. Me? I avoid malls at all cost. I'm a mail order and Internet shopper all the way. I'm not one to mix it up with the shoulder-to-shoulder mob scenes, the parking spot wars, hand gesturing, short tempers, overtired children, not to mention those who really do not like sitting on Santa's lap, despite their parents insistence that they do so.

Nevertheless, in recent years, I discovered his affinity for dealing with the traffic and the crowds on this final day. As it happened, I had completed my shopping in November. I had already inventoried everything, shipped the out of state packages and was in the process of wrapping the local ones, when I discovered there was a duplicate gift. It was too late to send it back for a replacement. I would have to make a local exchange. In order to see a smiling face come Christmas morning, it would mean a trip to the local mall to exchange it (cue the *Jaws* theme music). "I could get eaten alive in there," I thought. It's

Christmas Eve day! Parking will be a mess, all that pushing and shoving and jockeying for position. Who needs it! Maybe I could wait until after Christmas. After all the mental gymnastics, I decided to go for it.

First, I noticed most of the shoppers on this day are, for the most part, my husband's comrades, other men! He is not alone in this. But, Second, and most important, everyone is nice! The customers, as well as, those drawing the short straw and are working the registers on Christmas Eve! It's quite an interesting study in human nature. The shoppers have no room to complain, everybody, smiling! They have waited until the last minute. The employees seem genuinely at ease to have pleasant shoppers, without all the drama of the last several weeks. People are patient and kind.

It has always been a surprise to me how the Christmas season can bring out the worst in us when we are shopping or driving in all the holiday chaos. "Ma'am, the line is back there!" (With an eye roll or an off-color remark in faint whisper to a friend). Guilty as charged, I have fallen into the same trap. I do not like who I can become in those environments, so I avoid them, if possible. James warns us, "Out of the same mouth come praise and cursing. My brothers, this should not be." Yet, one day, I was witness to a modern-day Christmas miracle and the secret to my husband's attraction to his annual shopping tradition.

For a short time in my teenage years, I lived on a ranch. One of my chores was collecting the eggs from the hen house. I enjoyed this job. I loved to see the different shades of these fragile, although filthy eggs and visit the chickens. The hen house reeked of all things unmentionable, but it was wholesome smells I grew to respect and welcome. We ate what we grew or raised on the ranch. What we put in our mouth came from our own hand. And what came out of our mouth came from our own heart; hearts which grew bigger for God because of His Divine Providence for us from His Creation. We did not have a mall. We lived off the land and bartered for the rest. It was a powerful experience.

Jesus said, "What goes into a man's mouth does not make him 'unclean,' but what comes out of his mouth, that is what makes him 'unclean'" (Matt. 15:11). Like the eggs I gathered, words have the power to nourish or they can just be filthy little things, with life-giving and life-sustaining potential. Praise or cursing. It is a choice, a fragile choice.

Lord Jesus, please help us all to be mindful of the power of our own tongue. Help us to think before we speak. Be in our thoughts and our words, not just with our brothers and sisters in Christ, but with everyone, so that they will know that we are Your children. Let our words be beacons of light drawing people to You not driving them away. Keep us ever mindful that our words must glorify You and let us seek you in doing it, not just at Christmastime, but all year through. Finally, this Christmas help us to remember the true miracle of Christmas, Your birth. In Your name we pray, amen.

WEEKLY WISDOM WALK

Search and read every scripture containing both "mouth" and "words" this week! Enjoy.

Why dress yourself in scarlet and put on jewels of gold? Why shade your eyes with paint? You adorn yourself in vain (Jer. 4:30).

THE PERFECT CHRISTMAS TREE

Perfection, Vanity

What are you doing, O devastated one? Why dress yourself in scarlet and put on jewels of gold? Why shade your
eyes with paint? You adorn yourself in vain.
—JEREMIAH 4:30

"THIS IS *THE* one!" my husband exclaims with great conviction, all smiles, dimples gleaming, with great hope in his eyes, willing our adventure to be only so easy. And, so it begins—the hunt for the "perfect" Christmas tree. It is interesting to reflect on our twenty years of marriage and the many oscillations our hunt has cycled through. A perfectionist since childhood, I sought out the perfect tree early in our marriage, much to my husband's dismay. His unwavering love for me and desire to make my Christmas dreams finally come true were worth the cost of the muscle pain ointments he would require the following day, as every spruce and fir was picked up and pounded to the pavement for a sneak peak at the grandeur, which would result once adorned. When my son was young, this hailed tradition would take us to Christmas tree farms, fully equipped with hayrides, hot cider, and funnel cakes. But, years of intermittent droughts taught us the local building supply store is a far more reliable investment. Not that this stopped me from seeking the perfect triangle, no holes, and no gaps, just the right tip for the star, soft needles, and a plethora of other criteria.

The tree trimming has taken on its own story over the years. Early in our marriage, I did most of the trimming. Mike had little interest. I was in design school and really wanted a showpiece. In fact, we had no furniture. So, once a year, our first home had a stunning color coordinated, completely adorned, flocked and flickering fir of some sort. After our child was born, not much changed until our son was able to help with the decorations. Hmmm. A quandary! My love for him was so great, I had to give up my idealistic desires and leave the bottom rows for our child, who took great delight in tree trimming, just as I did, although with much more authenticity, I am quite sure. As he has grown, I have discovered more about this tradition through his innocent eyes. He has his favorite ornaments. Of course, my husband and I do as well, but it is most interesting to see them through the eyes of a child. They are rarely the ones you expect and for reasons you would never guess. Over time, our tradition has taken on new meaning, and believe it or not, my husband's great hope to leave with the first tree on the lot has often become our reality.

Yes, I still fuss over the "details" of the tree trimming. We play our Christmas music, light a cozy fire, pour the Eggnog and begin to place the special ornaments on the tree. Eventually, everyone has had enough, leaving the following day for me to add the "extra" and make the tree really "sing!" Usually, I am alone this day, so I spend some time gazing at my "perfect" tree and all it represents to me. I see the angels and the crosses and the ribbons and flowers interspersed with the homemade ornaments we've collected and created over the years, pets since past, toothless baby faces adjacent to those with full toothed grins.

The truth is there have been many Christmases I have spent alone. There were childhood Christmases filled with grief. I have longed to recapture Christmases past, but I cannot. No perfect tree will bring back lost time. My obsession over the adorning of a tree is futile and in vain. It is a façade, as so many of our decorations, to-do lists, parties, and extravagances tend to be. We lose sight of what we are doing and why we are truly doing it. Are we trying to recover something or to cover something? We need no fanfare, pomp, or circumstance to celebrate the arrival of our King. A simple Charlie Brown tree will do. Yet, like the harlot (Jerusalem) adorning herself with scarlet and gold, in desperation for a plight, a fate already secured, we pour our energy into extravagant machinations and wonder why our busyness robbed us of the ability to go deeply into relationship with our newborn King this season.

I tell myself, "This year, it's going to be different. I'm not falling into the trap again." I admit, I do improve. But one of these years, I'm going to get it right, not "perfect" but better. There is no perfect, only the One perfect King. I do not want to miss the celebration of His arrival lost in a box of golden baubles and scarlet ribbons, trying to recreate or recapture Christmases past.

As I caught the ellipse of rain drops clinging to a scarlet tree devoid of leaves one winter evening, I watched as the last light reflected through the water droplets as if to twinkle and dance. This tree was every bit as beautiful as my ornamented version, chopped down from its wood. Yet, like our Jesus, it is alive and brings hope of new life next spring, reminding me of the Holy One who promises to fill our emptiness. Who came to do so! And they brought Him gold, frankincense, and myrrh. There was no splish-splash, no fanfare. There was a simple birth, three gifts, a bright star, and an angel on one remarkable night. May our Christmases this year be more about Him and less about us.

Precious Lord Jesus, I praise You, the King of Kings, Lord of Lords who came to us in a simple, imperfect setting, which became the cradle for all humanity. Let this be the year my heart, mind, and soul are entirely focused on You. Let us all be reminded of the simplicity of Your birth and come to adore You, Christ the newborn King, without to-do lists, agendas, and burdens of busyness preventing us from missing moments to praise Your name. Amen.

Weekly Wisdom Walk

Don't we all get caught up in the fanfare of Christmastime? What is it for you? The endless Christmas party commitments? Open House expectations? Traditions that have simply gotten out of hand over the years? Is it time to throttle back? Have you asked yourself why you do it? Who is this for? Is it for me? The family? The children? Are you filling something? Avoiding something? Is there any pride or vanity involved at all? Take these questions to our Father this year before beginning the annual rituals. You may be surprised at the answers. Challenge yourself to do all things to glorify Jesus this year, Him alone. "Whatever you do, work at it with all your heart, as working for the Lord, not for men, since you know that you will receive an inheritance from the Lord as a reward. It is the Lord Christ you are serving" (Col. 3:23–24).

The virgin will be with child and will give birth to a son, and they will call him "Immanuel" (Matt. 1:23).

BREAKING THE ICE

Thirst for Peace

The virgin will be with child and will give birth to a son, and
they will call him "Immanuel"—which means "God with us."
—MATTHEW 1:23

OH COME, OH Come Emmanuel"—my favorite Christmas carol, occupying many special moments over the years. One year, it became the reminder of God's presence after months of wandering in silence, seemingly without Him. The familiar hymn traversed my mind at first, faintly, from a distance until, finally, fully present consuming my thoughts only later to be sung in monastic chant during a silent retreat. I was desperately seeking reconnection with my Savior, who made a powerful reentry in my life during that particular Advent season, or at least I broke through the ice I had placed between us.

"...And ransom captive Israel." Each year is different. New verses resonate for me. I begin to understand the magnitude of what God did for us out of His great love. The ransom He paid to free His people. I, once a captive, shackled, cold with pride, hatred, and anger, was set free in a moment of forgiveness, first modeled by this Babe, Immanuel, Jesus—"God with us"—born to us a Savior.

"...That mourns in lovely exile here." I have learned the cost of unforgivingness, persecution, prolonged mourning, grief, and judgment, and my heart breaks for those still living in exile, self-inflicted or otherwise, because they do not know our Lord Jesus or only know a mere trickle of Him and have chosen to exist in exile from Him. I long for them to truly "see the Son of God appear" and "Rejoice! Rejoice!"

"Oh, come, our wisdom from on high." Why is it for many of us celebrating

Christmas with our families, we are least likely to find her—wisdom? Family dysfunction and petty differences slither into our warm and cozy picture post-card gatherings of ornamented trees, festive foods, stockings hung with care above curled up family pets snuggling next to crackling fireplaces to keep the chill of new fallen snow at bay. Yet the icy chill creeps inside with us unawares, tensions rise, and wisdom is abated.

"...to us the path of knowledge show, and teach us in her ways to go." For some, our "not so finest hours" have occurred during Christmastime. We allow the stress of what the world's expectations have placed on the celebra-tion of the Christ child to drive our choices and behaviors. We emote based on worldly decisions vs. heavenly ones. We no longer seek wise counsel. We allowed wisdom's escape weeks ago. We long to get back on the path of knowl-edge to seek out divine direction. Yet, our path has become a frozen lake, slick and slippery, too treacherous to traverse alone. We yearn for a Savior to show us the way.

"Oh, come desire of nations bind. In one the hearts of all mankind; Oh, bid our sad divisions cease. And, be yourself, our King of Peace." While I have traveled countries and find it hard to believe many still live in nations of polit-ical, economic, social, and religious unrest, I believe we worship a mighty God whose desire is to bind our hearts together as one, and we are to go out and make disciples of all nations. I hope my child will be alive to see our Savior, the living water, the delight of every heart that beats. Still, I know this division cannot be bound unless we begin in our own homes. One Christmas without division, hearts afire, with all wisdom and knowledge guiding our collective paths—breaking through the icy winter's chill, agendas aside, no discord, with freedom from hurry sickness, control, pride, short fuses, and unattainable expectations.

Each year, our families age and grow larger. Each year, the challenge seems more daunting. We need wisdom, guidance, and knowledge. We need a Savior to accomplish such a feat. A Savior, born of a virgin—*God with us.* This Christmas, let it be the year, Emmanuel comes to you without the bitter chill of past pains, mistakes and missteps, but with hearts on fire for the One who restores life. No longer captive or in exile. He has paid your ransom. Welcome, indeed, celebrate the King of Peace. "Rejoice! Rejoice!"

> *Blessed Lord Jesus, we welcome You into our hearts and our home.*
> *Please help us to keep a heavenly perspective on the tremendous gift*
> *of Your birth, especially this Advent season. Oh, Come, Oh Come,*
> *Immanuel into our lives, every corner, every tradition. Allow Your*

warmth, Your peace and Your pace to rest upon us. Melt away the chill of winter, literally and figuratively, with Your restorative love. And, in all that we do, let it glorify You. Thank You for being our Savior. In You and for You, we rejoice, amen.

Weekly Wisdom Walk

Do you have the best intentions to make each Christmas special, unhurried, warm, and memorable, only to look back and wonder what happened? If so, start praying and planning now about what you can do differently. What can be eliminated, added, or replaced. Time-consuming traditions replaced by more meaningful ones. Is Christmas difficult for you because of a lost loved one? Loneliness? Family dysfunction? Finances? How can you apply biblical principles to make this season a new experience?

Glory to God in the highest, and on earth peace to men on whom his favor rests (Luke 2:14).

WHITE CHRISTMAS

Peace

"Today in the town of David a Savior has been born to you; he is Christ
the Lord. This will be a sign to you: You will find a baby wrapped in
cloths and lying in a manger." Suddenly a great company of the heavenly
host appeared with the angel, praising God and saying, "Glory to God
in the highest, and on earth peace to men on whom his favor rests."
—LUKE 2:11–14

HOW MANY TIMES have you heard the Christmas story? Each year we
read it to ourselves, have it read to us, or read it to others hoping
to find something new and fresh in this most miraculous telling on
which our entire Christian faith hinges. If there were no birth, there would be
no sacrifice. There would be no entry into a fallen world of our Prince of Peace,
our Savior, who would give His life for our sin only thirty-three years later and
wash us white as snow. Glory to God, indeed! And, on Earth, peace! The Prince
of Peace!

Yet, why is peace so elusive? We have peace availed to us in a person, in Jesus
Christ, who came to us more than two thousand years ago and was prophesied
about long beforehand, "For to us a child is born, to us a son is given, and the
government will be on his shoulders. And he will be called Wonderful Counselor, Mighty God, Everlasting Father, Prince of Peace" (Isa. 9:6). When have
you known true peace? How many times? Can you count them? Did it exist
over a period of years or in specific highlights, ethereal moments, fleeting?

Some may equate peace to tranquility, calm, and silence. For others, it's
quite the contrary. In my youth, following a tumultuous childhood, I used to
find peace only in noise and chaos. As soon as I would come home, I turned on

the TV or the stereo, friends came by, and the phone would ring. Somehow, it quieted the noise in my head, the shouting, the images of violence, the madness and unrest from a past I was desperately trying to drown out with chatter and clamor. Peace, for me, came with an ever-increasing volume. Once I found healing in my Savior, the noise was no longer necessary. I married, had a child, and relished the quiet. Peace evaded me on many a sleepless night, yet when serenity and harmony fell upon us; I caught glimpses of peace, however fleeting and worldly.

As I have grown in my faith, I have sought out peace as one might seek fine treasure. I spend time alone deep in thought and ponder the ways of the world. I've traveled to war-torn countries. I have talked with soldiers on furlough for the holidays waiting to be reunited with wives and new babies they're meeting for the first time before heading back to fight for peace. I've listened to family and friends squabble for peace in their relationships.

We continue to wrestle with peace as if it were something attainable through a physical action within our control. If only I were married, I would finally find the peace I am looking for. If only I could have the child I have always wanted. If only I had a different job. If only I could have been born into different circumstances. If only I were not a part of this war. It was not my choice. If only this did not happen to me. If only (fill in the blank). The truth is our peace is not found in our circumstances. Our peace lies in a person. In Jesus Christ, born to us a Savior, no matter the circumstances. Our peace lies in the midst of the noise, despite the noise. We can have peace in the middle of complete chaos or in the quietest tranquil setting, and it will feel and sound the same. It is a peace that emanates from the inside, not from the outside.

My husband asked me to marry him on Christmas Eve. What began as a rainy day, ended in the most beautiful snowfall. I had prayed for a white Christmas, because we did not see too many of those in Texas. My prayers were answered, and we took an evening walk in the new, freshly fallen snow. Not a soul was outside. It was just he and I amidst a quaint neighborhood in the snow-laden pines of the Northeast. The snowflakes were large and the branches were heavy. If we stood still, we could almost hear them make the faintest of sounds. This was about as close as I had ever come to feeling peace. And yet, even this amazing man, the most picture postcard setting, and the happiest day of my life were a poor substitute for an awesome Savior.

True peace comes not from a situation. Circumstances are fleeting. True peace comes from a person, a baby, born to us a Savior, wrapped in clothes and lying in a manger. "Glory to God in the highest, and on earth peace...'" (Luke 2:14).

Lord Jesus, We praise You for coming to us as Savior of the world. Let us find new meaning and renewed hope in the story of Your birth. For so many of us, this season can be the least peaceful. The irony is perplexing. Draw us to You. Lord and replenish us with Your peace, the peace that surpasses all understanding and emanates from within. In the midst of chaos, let us be calm and unshakeable, in the turmoil of expectation; let us have complete clarity and tranquility. Focus our energy fully on Your restorative power, immeasurable love and peace everlasting. Amen.

Weekly Wisdom Walk

Reread the story of Jesus' birth. Try reading it in each of the Gospels. Choose a favorite version. Find something new about the story, perhaps a phrase resonating differently. You might also try reading the story, considering the perspective of one of the biblical persons, Mary maybe or a shepherd. Breathe new life in this miraculous story and share it with others. Merry Christmas!

He covers the face of the full moon, spreading his clouds over it (Job 26:9).

COMPREHENDING GOD

Motives

He covers the face of the full moon, spreading his clouds over it.
—JOB 26:9

I LOVE THE BOOK of Job. It is so much more than the word of God breathed into poetic prose. To me, it is the most wise and accurate depiction of human nature available to us. I see myself in the story everywhere, in each character. I've been the know-it-all friend, as well as, the young one in the room listening in disbelief at all I was hearing, yet not quite sure I should speak up for fear I would be dismissed due to my age. I have defended myself to others with righteous indignation as our victor, Job, with less a platform on which to stand and far less credible an argument.

I also love the story for the intellectual conversation. I have participated in numerous Bible studies and groups over the years, and for me, there is nothing like a great riveting debate over what it all means. Not just literal content, but the subjective, the whole lot of it. I like to read the work of apologetics, those who commit their time to the very defense of the origins and authority of Christianity. I love to discuss the key points of Christian literature and unpack the classics; particularly those that make the top-ten Christian book lists.

I always believed my affinity for devouring Scripture and Christian literature, reveling in any degree of discussion about it, was because I thirst for knowledge. I love the intellectual heart of a matter versus, simply, the heart of it, which does not seem to be enough. Recently, I came to a more relevant conclusion. I think I just want to be right.

On some level, I believe there is a group of us who truly want to believe we have God all figured out. Like Eliphaz, Bildad, and Zophar, we want to know why things are the way they are, what God is up to, why and when He speaks, how and when He acts, when our circumstances are by God's hand, our own hand, or just life. Sometimes, we may even have convinced ourselves (fooled, more likely) that we are acting in another's best interests by sharing such wisdom. It's a delusion, albeit a pacifying one, to believe we understand our circumstances. In this way, the fear of the unknown is bound and vanquished, and a sense of security drapes over us, as if God himself were reassuring our enlightenment with a heavenly hug.

The problem arises when we cannot convince our subject that, indeed, we have achieved total comprehension of the situation. Therein lays the rub. We have often heard the terminology, "the patience of Job," which mostly refers to Job's endurance, his suffering. This is a man, blameless and upright, though still a sinner, who persevered through great loss to his property, family, business, physical health, and social standing. In fact, the lesson of his circumstance might better be referenced "the perseverance of Job." To me, patience is a word more fitting for the deep well Job had to draw from in dealing with his supposed friends.

Ultimately, Job loses his patience, though. He cracks. And, with a vein of sarcasm, he responds with a, "Wow, this is *great* wisdom. Thanks, guys! With friends like you, who needs enemies?" (or something along those lines). Job, then, proceeds to take another stab at defending himself and explaining God to the three friends, who seem to, however misguided, have the Maker of the universe all figured out!

Like the most-learned professor, Bible scholar, preacher, or intellectual, Job, too, falls shy of capturing the essence of who God is, but he makes one important point we could all relearn. In a series of powerful descriptions, he manages to make the point that God is incomprehensible. "He spreads out the northern skies over empty space; he suspends the earth over nothing. He wraps up the waters in his clouds, yet the clouds do not burst under their weight. He covers the face of the full moon, spreading his clouds over it" (Job 26:7–9).

Have we forgotten? How great is our God? Do I think I know because He has done amazing, even miraculous things in my life? Yes! But, I am limited only to the extent of what He has shown me. I will not know the fullness of His Majesty until Christ comes again. "Now we see but a poor reflection as in a mirror; then we shall see face to face. Now I know in part; then I shall know fully, even as I am fully known" (1 Cor. 13:12). In our arrogance, so manifest in the words of Job's friends, we believe our experiences have given us clarity, yet we see through the glass dimly and easily forget. We cannot comprehend the greatness of our God, not even by reading God's own response to Job.

I like to write what I have experienced and what I have learned, but more importantly, I like to paint a picture with words about what God allows me to think and dream through ordinary encounters with Him. It is a daily journey. Whether I am reading His word, the work of others, walking in His creation, serving, worshipping, singing, feeling praiseful or grateful, debating or retreating—I am still learning, trying to soak up more of Him. I will never reach the fullness and richness of complete understanding. Sometimes I need to be reminded. Comprehending God was never my goal. There is time, a season for that. For now, I will just walk with Him and be grateful our extraordinary God has invited ordinary me into relationship with Him. This is my prayer for you as well.

> *Almighty Father, You are the One and only God, sovereign over all. Forgive our arrogance when we believe we have all of the answers, then look upward at the full moon and marvel at its majesty. Remind us of Your omnipotence every time we encounter a situation, which seems impossible. Hold our tongues when we feel a need to intellectualize an answer for it. Help us to find You with our hearts and not with our heads. Keep our hearts open and pliable to receive You. Renew a right spirit within us that glorifies You. Walk with us, Lord, each day, in the way everlasting. In Jesus' name, amen.*

Weekly Wisdom Walk

Read the Book of Job. If you have a copy of *The Message*, it might be a good translation to use as it reads more like a story without interruption from notes and verse demarcations. Find yourself in the story. Make notes about any thoughts or epiphanies you may have. Take a walk with our mighty God and lift your revelations up to Him. Reflect back over the year of study. Ask God to reveal to you what area(s) for you to direct your focus, as we approach the New Year. Lift these up in prayer. Notice the ordinary, made by the Extraordinary, your heavenly Father.

To Contact the Author

kzmarotta@aol.com

or

www.blessedbybosnia.blogspot.com

Proceeds from this books' sales will go to the Evangelical Church in Capljina, Bosnia. Visit their website at www.evangelica.ba